FOLD
in the
CHEESE

FOLD IN THE CHEESE.
Copyright © 2022 by Hollan Publishing.
All rights reserved.
Printed in China.
No part of this book may be used or reproduced
in any manner whatsoever without written
permission except in the case of reprints in the
context of reviews.

Andrews McMeel Publishing
a division of Andrews McMeel Universal
1130 Walnut Street, Kansas City, Missouri 64106

www.andrewsmcmeel.com

22 23 24 25 26 SDB 10 9 8 7 6 5 4 3 2 1

ISBN: 978-1-5248-7531-2

Library of Congress Control Number: 2022933959

Illustrations by Joanna Price
Editor: Jennifer Calvert
Art Director: Katie Jennings Campbell
Cover Design: Joanna Price
Interior Design: Noora Cox
Production Editor: Brianna Westervelt
Production Manager: Chadd Keim

Andrews McMeel books are available at
quantity discounts with bulk purchase for
educational, business, or sales promotional use.
For information, please e-mail the Andrews
McMeel Publishing Special Sales Department:
specialsales@amuniversal.com.

FOLD
in the
CHEESE

AN UNOFFICIAL GUIDE TO
Splendiferous Entertaining
For Fans of $chitt's Creek

Written by Parker Long
Illustrated by Joanna Price

Andrews McMeel
PUBLISHING®

CONTENTS

⚜WELCOME⚜

Whether they're throwing ostentatious soirées or Valium-fueled tantrums, entertaining a crowd (or sometimes just Stevie) is what the Roses do best! Let their sagacious advice and biting wit wash over you with *Fold in the Cheese.* This splendiferous compilation of tips, recipes, scene references, and party-planning peccadillos takes its inspiration from the wise and worldly owners of the best little town in . . . Canada? Probably Canada.

Learn how to put on a proper games night, host a holiday party, and organize your own movie premiere, all while balancing your caviar dreams with your disappointingly dairy-filled reality. Folded in among these careful instructions are a smattering of delicious Rose-family-inspired food and cocktail recipes you can whip up for guests. Make this year's murder-mystery night a memorable one with your signature Crime of Passion cocktail. Master the grill with Hundred-Dollar Sliders. Surprise your inamorata with a delectable Chocolate Ganache Torte Cake. This illustrious tome gives you everything you need to make your events . . . memorable.

Best wishes for your entertaining success!

chapter

1

Towny PARTIES

Whether you're throwing a backyard soirée, a woodsy gathering, or an intimate little bash at a charming farmette, the tenets of any good towny party are the same: thoughtful guest list, palatable refreshments, and a basic code of conduct regarding romance. Of course, you (like David) may need to lower your standards, depending on the quality of the townspeople in attendance. But you can make any town gathering better by releasing all expectations and going with the flow of the evening. You may be inspired to drink from a beer bong, partake in some contraband, or have a heart-to-heart with an ex. Just enjoy yourself! You might be surprised by where the evening leads you.

⟩ TAILGATES

If your journey should take you to a tailgate in the woods, maintain some cautious optimism. Pint glasses and dignified conversation may not be in your future, but you might be surprised by how much you enjoy being chanted at while chugging lukewarm beer. Just be sure to dress comfortably and attend the party with friends who are more familiar with the towny-rich environment. They can walk you through the finer points of beer-pong etiquette and point out which handsome, shirtless locals are already spoken for (if you give them the chance).

Know Your Audience

When invited to partake in a tailgate party, it's best to ask a local what to expect. Should you opt to host such an event, you would surely offer high-end wines and beautifully grilled canapés to enjoy over gas-flame fire features. But no one really "hosts" a tailgate, do they? Like swallows to Capistrano, sketchy locals are as inexplicably drawn to bonfires and kegs as their ancestors. So the best you can do is get a clear picture of what you're in for, from the drunken marshmallow roasting to the shocking abundance of flannel.

Embrace the Vibe

Once you know what the evening is likely to hold, you can adjust your expectations accordingly. That means dressing warmly on a fall evening in the woods and sticking close to friends. This isn't a Manhattan club—flying solo in stilettos is probably not the best choice for a patchy field full of strangers. Let yourself be caught up in the rustic pleasures of the evening. Until you don't want to any more. Knowing when to leave people wanting more is an art form (and one that Alexis has perfected).

BARN PARTIES

Unlike a tailgate, a barn party can offer just a hint of understated elegance. And that hint of elegance is you. String all the globe lights you want, nothing about using a barn as a venue is particularly sophisticated. What it is is a venue in which you can wear your littlest black dress, drink alcohol out of a plastic cup, and eat chips and dip in lighting just good enough to see hot, flannel-clad townies smiling at you from across the room. In other words, it's the best place to meet someone under the age of fifty in a small town.

Follow a Code of Conduct

Parties held in spaces where animals or heavy machinery once resided don't require much in the way of a dress code. But there's really no such thing as being overdressed in a room that contains your ex and the person they're currently dating, who happens to look unnaturally good in a basic white tee. Whatever you do, resist the urge to compete for a guy like David and Stevie do. The last thing you want is to end up being some (ruggedly handsome) narcissist's sloppy seconds.

Avoid Rustic Refreshments

A venue can be rustic. Refreshments, however, should meet basic standards of hygiene and flavor. That means a degree of separation between any veggies and the compost with which they're grown, and ice made with filtered water and not well water. (In an ideal world, any ice you serve your guests would be made using water that's hand-collected from melting glaciers.) And as barn parties are a target-rich environment, snacks should be light and pleasant-smelling. No one wants to hook up with someone shoveling garlic hummus into their mouth in a dark corner. Well, no one except Jake, and he has some very questionable standards.

TROPICAL THEME PARTIES

The crown jewel in the mesmerizing assortment of towny parties is an annual backyard bash where decorum and laws become mere suggestions.

The small-town luau is a lovely little piece of paradise featuring plastic leis, colorful shirts, tiki torches, loose morals, and an entire pig rotating on a spit. Adding a flowing cheese fountain and a little grass can go a long way toward forging lasting friendships between you and your guests.

Be Inclusive

The backyard soirée is a great opportunity to ingratiate yourself with the regular people of your town. You never know when those relationships may come in handy, like when running for town council or trying to pull off a wedding under emergency circumstances. So don't count anyone out when creating your guest list. The true hallmark of a towny party is that it's open to one and all—regardless of your feelings about the "all."

Institute Some Age Limits

Although you can't be held accountable for the number of fake IDs in proliferation, the underage towny is far less of a concern than your parents showing up at a party of your peers. Especially when that party contains promising dating prospects. Let your elders know that, although you love them, you have no desire to see them dance in public.

Offer Alcohol Alternatives

Another hallmark of a towny party? Libations. Few can stomach an all-inclusive gathering without some sort of social lubricant to facilitate conversations and to encourage budding friendships to blossom. Obviously, you should have water and some sort of sparkling beverage for those who choose to be heroes. But offering some relaxing plant-based substances can be a nice touch, especially where grass skirts are involved. (It helps if the Law is the one bringing those substances.)

Hawaiian Pork Sandwiches

This recipe gives you all the flavor of a Hawaiian-themed soirée even if you don't have a backyard large enough to roast a whole pig. Or a backyard. Or an oven. All you really need are your wits, a 6-quart slow cooker, a saucepan, and a ride to the grocery store.

≫ SERVES 6

1 (4-pound) boneless pork shoulder

½ cup low-sodium soy sauce

1½ cups low-sodium chicken stock

1 cup pineapple juice

½ cup ketchup

¼ cup brown sugar

2 tablespoons minced garlic

1 tablespoon minced fresh ginger

1 tablespoon cornstarch

3 tablespoons water

1 cup diced pineapple

12 mini Hawaiian rolls

1. Trim the fat from the pork shoulder (or, better yet, ask a neighbor to do it) and place it in the slow cooker.

2. In a medium bowl, whisk together the soy sauce, chicken stock, pineapple juice, ketchup, brown sugar, garlic, and ginger. Pour the mixture over the pork, put the lid on the slow cooker, and let everything cook on LOW for 8 hours or on HIGH for 5 hours.

3. Once the pork shoulder is cooked through (meaning it has an internal temperature of at least 145°F, as conveyed by a meat thermometer), transfer it to a cutting board.

4. Add half of the liquid from the slow cooker to a medium saucepan and discard the rest. Let the liquid come to a boil over medium-high heat.

5. In a small bowl, whisk together the cornstarch and water. Once the sauce has come to a boil, whisk in the cornstarch mixture. Let the sauce keep boiling until thick enough to coat the back of a spoon.

6. Meanwhile, use two forks to shred the pork shoulder. Transfer the shredded pork to a large bowl and stir in the pineapple and the thickened sauce to combine.

7. Divide the pork among the rolls and serve to guests and ravenous family members.

chapter

2

Backyard BARBECUES

Whether you receive a sweet gesture from a partner marking a relationship milestone or make a startlingly unexpected home-run hit, a barbecue can be just the thing to celebrate your unlikeliest accomplishments. There's no better feeling than enjoying large quantities of food with people you love . . . and a few you tolerate. Hosting a barbecue may seem so simple that a monkey—or even Roland—could pull it off, but these events require more than just an experienced grill master. (Having one of those is pretty much nonnegotiable, though.) From extending the invitations to timing your meal, you'll have a lot more than perfectly grilled sliders on your plate. Like, for example, potato salad.

⟩ INVITATIONS

First things first: invite your guests. Although larger barbecues can accommodate drop-ins, intimate backyard gatherings require some structure. If you expect any guests to contribute substantially to the afternoon, get a firm RSVP. Follow up with the guest of honor to ensure he actually received his invite, preferably while avoiding the words "charred meat" and "carnies." And remember that, when it comes to a small family barbecue, "the more the merrier" is not always an appropriate sentiment. At the very least, make sure you get a full dating history from any unexpected plus-ones.

⟩ TIMING YOUR MEAL

Planning any event requires choosing a date and time that work for the majority of your guests. But planning an event centered on food comes with its own set of considerations. Will your grill master be able to attend? Will the meal act as a reward for hard work? Will its timing and activities trigger any recent traumas? You can't know the answers to all of these questions, but they should at least cross your mind during those first optimistic moments when the idea of grilling food without the help of a personal chef pops into your head.

Day of the Week

The date you choose for your barbecue will depend heavily on guest availability and the cooperation of the weather. But you should also take into consideration such intangibles as the meat-processing schedules of any local farms. Hearing the terrified screams of pigs is sure to put even the most pitiless among you off their pork chops. (David would say that this is also just one of many arguments for having a strong selection of side dishes on your picnic table.)

Time of Day

You may be used to a more worldly dining schedule, but your guests will expect the food to be ready at a reasonable hour. Choose a time that works for everyone and that considers the last time people enjoyed a meal so that they're not ravenous enough to eat the decorations. Should you let the event extend into the evening hours, you might enjoy a fireside sing-along led by a butter-voiced guest. And no one wants that. So set a firm cutoff point as well as a sensible dining time.

Embrace Joy

Losing everything and landing in a town with even less can make you appreciate the little things that are actually a big deal (like a celebratory cookie on your anniversary). Although some momentous occasions lend themselves to momentous events, barbecues are perfect for celebrating these smaller moments. Take the time to savor them while you're savoring that pasta salad.

As Motivation

The promise of a freshly grilled lunch and the smell of that lunch wafting over, say, home plate, can be hugely motivating for some people. Should you have one of these people in your life and need their help—with a competition or, really, any kind of manual labor—plan your barbecue post-favor. And hope for just enough of a breeze in the forecast to entice your food-focused friend without entirely distracting them from the task at hand.

》 EQUIPMENT

As simple as the act of grilling may be, it relies on a little more than skill. You don't need bells and whistles (or even a built-in wine fridge, like Johnny's used to), but you do need a grill that isn't full of unintentional kindling ready to burst into flame at the first drop of hot grease. It would be great if your burgers didn't taste like burnt rust. And make sure you ask for help if you don't know what the hell you're doing.

Cleanliness

It goes without saying that anything you cook food on should be clean, but you may have to make do with equipment that's in less-than-ideal condition. You would be amazed at what you can do when you apply a little elbow grease to a grill that's seen better days. You know what works even better than scrubbing a rusted grill clean? Replacing it with a similar but suspiciously rust-free grill like the show's producers absolutely did for Roland. But barring that, yeah, elbow grease.

Handling

If you're not the most confident griller, you may have to rely on the kindness (and patience) of guests to get that perfect medium-rare slider. Never be too proud to admit that you have no earthly idea what you're doing when food is involved. It's a public service, really. Have someone knowledgeable walk you through things like lighting the briquettes and searing the meat. And no matter how comfortable you are in front of a grill, avoid cooking shirtless. (Unless you have six-pack abs that glow in the firelight. Alexis would consider that a public service, too.)

❯ APPROPRIATE BARBECUE FARE

No matter the size of, or reason for, the barbecue, there's no need to break out the filet mignon. Even the Roses can appreciate a hard-won hamburger or hot dog. And it's really for the best if you don't serve bacon to guests who may have recently been traumatized by the sounds of pigs meeting their maker. Just buy the best-quality meat you can afford, and enough of it to satisfy your hungriest guest's appetite. (So, if they're anything like David, a lot.) You can also offer a smattering of sides to offset the cost of buying copious amounts of meat.

How to Grill Like a Pro (or Roland)

Of course you know how to grill. This is just a little basic refresher . . . for other people . . . who might not know how to grill. Or for those who are used to working with knobs and tanks instead of briquettes.

You'll Need

Charcoal grill • Grill brush
Charcoal briquettes • Lighter fluid • Matches
Vegetable oil • Steel tongs

1. **CLEAN THE GRILL**
   Make sure the grill is in food-safe condition. Remove any abandoned birds' nests, cobwebs, and ash before using a grill brush to scrape the grates clean. (A little water and dish soap can also go a long way.)

2. **LIGHT THE BRIQUETTES**
   Pour the charcoal into the belly of your grill and shape it into a mound. Add a little lighter fluid and let the briquettes soak that up for 20 seconds. Then toss in a lit match. (Carefully, though. You wouldn't want to lose your eyebrows.)

3. **PREP THE GRILL**
   Move the hot coals over to one side of the grill to create zones for direct and indirect heat and brush the grill grates with a bit of vegetable oil to season them.

4. **COOK THE MEAT**
   Use direct heat to cook anything you want to see sear marks on and indirect heat for tougher cuts of meat. Turn your food only once during cooking, and do not press on your burgers. If you don't have someone to tell you when the burgers are done, use a meat thermometer to make sure the meat hits at least 145°F.

BEYOND THE GRILL

Johnny coming home with $100 worth of meat is all well and good, but guests will need more than that and your good intentions to fill their growling stomachs. A barbecue is nothing if not a smorgasbord of delicious offerings. Creamy side dishes, thirst-quenching beverages, and an array of toppings are a must. Condiments can be controversial, but always make sure you have the Big Three: ketchup, mustard, and mayo. (Yes, mayo. It's Canada. Probably.)

Offer a Smattering of Sides

When hosting a small barbecue, you can stick to the basic salads everyone expects to see alongside burgers and hot dogs: potato, pasta, and macaroni. And yes, those last two are very different things. At a large barbecue, don't hesitate to ask guests to bring their favorites. The important thing is to have something for everyone and fully embrace the abundance of comfort food. You never know who'll need it.

Don't Forget Dessert

Some might say dessert is even more important than the meal. Offer something everyone can share and not, for example, an oversized cookie. (It may be large, but that doesn't make it shareable.) There's nothing quite like ice cream to add a cool touch to a hot summer barbecue. One large tub of ice cream can serve several guests . . . or one very upset family member. Maybe have a backup tub.

Hundred-Dollar Sliders

Now that you A) have a working grill and B) know how to use it, you can make delicious sliders like the type of person who would have not one, not two, but three grill-themed aprons. Sauces, spices, and colorful accompaniments turn miniature hamburgers into a meal worthy of the Roses.

» SERVES 6

½ pound ground chuck
½ pound ground sirloin
1 tablespoon steak sauce
1 tablespoon Worcestershire sauce
2 teaspoons onion flakes
1 teaspoon garlic powder
1 teaspoon freshly ground black pepper

¾ teaspoon salt
3 slices favorite cheese, halved
1 large tomato, sliced
1 small handful of greens
12 dill pickle slices
6 seeded slider rolls

1. Add the ground beef, steak sauce, Worcestershire sauce, and all the spices to a medium bowl, and use clean hands or a spatula to combine everything.

2. Divide the seasoned meat into 6 patties. Lightly press a thumb into the center of each patty to make an indentation (this will help the patties stay flat).

3. Heat a gas or charcoal grill to 450°F. Grill the sliders for about 2 minutes on one side, then gently flip and move them to a spot over indirect heat. For medium-rare sliders, grill the patties for an additional 4 minutes, topping each with cheese 1 minute before they finish grilling.

4. Let the meat rest for 2 minutes before building your burgers with your choice of tomatoes, greens, and pickles on slider rolls.

chapter

3

Dinner PARTIES

Few things seem more straightforward than a gathering of friends and family over a homecooked meal. These exclusive little parties are not to be underestimated, though. The humble dinner party can serve many purposes, from getting to know new friends to settling important business matters. One thing is for sure: you'll leave the table knowing your dinner companions far better than you did when you sat down. One might even say you'll know too much. Whether you're hoping to end the party with a signed contract, a slapped face, or a rousing game of Hedbanz, you'll need to give the evening and its events some serious thought. A little planning can save what's left of your sanity.

❯❯ HOSTING AN EVENING

Hosting a dinner party is far more perilous an endeavor than attending one. You'll need to navigate such emotional landmines as secret crushes, troubled relationships, inappropriate remarks, and lactose intolerance. One thing that can help avoid any upsets is being very clear with guests about your intentions for the evening. Like telling them how many people you've actually invited.

As long as you plan the evening thoughtfully, keep topics of conversation light, and help everyone set reasonable expectations, you should be . . . fine.

Keep an Eye on the Exits

Always have an elegant excuse to leave at the ready when dining with others. You could feign a migraine or pick a fight with a lover, to offer two tried-and-true examples. Such excuses should generally be reserved for when you're not hosting the evening, but sometimes, you do what you have to do.

Invite Guests Thoughtfully

With such an intimate gathering, it's important to be mindful of who you invite to your dinner table. Really consider whether watching them eat will be a worthwhile trade-off for the pleasure of their company. Ask yourself whether you can achieve your goals by some other means—ones that don't involve food. And make sure you fully understand the romantic dynamics of any couples you invite. Once you're absolutely sure about your choices—like, really sure—take a page out of Ted's book and make everyone a handwritten place card. It's just a nice touch.

Plan the Menu Accordingly

What you serve for dinner and appetizers will set the tone for the entire evening. A frozen lasagna flown in from out of state rather than lovingly handmade might create an environment of mistrust. (Or maybe that's just

Alexis and Mutt.) A cheeseball that elicits inappropriate confessions about a couple's sex life, for example, might make guests uncomfortable. But a casserole dish filled with delicious, hot, artery-clogging cheese? Now that spells dinner party success. (Warning: Do not serve a guest who is at risk of a cardiac event ten pounds of cheese. Don't. It doesn't end well for anyone.)

Prioritize Refreshments

When you're hosting, make sure your guests have a drink in their hands by the time they sit down. Even better, hand them a glass at the door. Make assumptions about their beverage preferences. It's fine. If everyone's going to make it through this night with their sanity intact, they might need a stiff drink to take the edge off. And for your teetotaler guests, be sure to have some nonalcoholic options available, too. As a guest, make sure you BYOB of choice. And if it doesn't make it into your glass by dinnertime, follow Moira's lead and gently remind your busy host that your house gift is there for the drinking. Now.

Eat with Decorum

As the host of the evening, it's your responsibility to set an example for the sort of behavior you hope to see from your guests. In a perfect world, that example would elevate the evening for all involved. So do not—and this cannot be emphasized enough—put your fingers in the fondue. In fact, maybe avoid finger foods altogether. There's absolutely nothing wrong with preparing food that requires the use of utensils. And then *requiring* the use of those utensils.

 BEING A COURTEOUS GUEST

When you find yourself invited into the home of a new, rather bumptious acquaintance, your first instinct may be to decline. Trust that instinct. But if it becomes clear that declining is not an option, graciously accept your host's hospitality. You certainly wouldn't want to insult anyone, after all.

In fact, compliment your host's home and decorating prowess. Whether they drew their inspiration from magazines like Jocelyn or bought an entire showroom like Ted, their pride in their home should blind them to any blatantly obvious awkwardness you're experiencing while being in it.

❯ DOING BUSINESS AT THE TABLE

Few get-togethers are as fraught as a dinner party used for business or information gathering. Not only do you have to account for a variety of personalities, but you also have to tolerate even the most unappetizing of eating habits. Surely it would have been simpler to grab a quick signature without getting dairy-based food products involved. But if you're forced to cut a deal over dinner, you can at least strive for a balance between business and . . . pleasure.

Do Your Research

Knowing who you're doing business with *before* you have to watch them laugh at lewd jokes with a mouth full of pigs-in-a-blanket could potentially save you from years of night terrors. Avoid that awkward situation by gathering as much information as you can before sitting down to dinner. Is this person really as liquid as you were led to believe or just having a midlife crisis? Are they literally the worst human being you've ever met? Are you rushing this deal for the right reasons? These are the kinds of questions to ask before extending an invite.

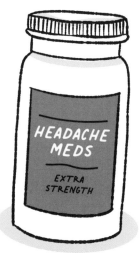

Seize Your Opportunity

Some might say you should ease into any business discussions after dinner. Those who say that are wrong. Get that fucking signature during cocktail hour—preferably even before you're browbeaten into that ill-fated dinner. Too much can go wrong between the martinis and the Easy Mac. Slap the host if you have to. Skip the negotiations, however appealing it might be to stick it to your human dumpster fire of a buyer. Just get it done.

Extra Cheesy Mac

When you're not at risk of giving your guest of honor a heart attack or an upset stomach, super-creamy mac and cheese can really hit the spot. It's the sort of good, home-cooked meal you expect from someone like Jocelyn, who always strives to show her dinner guests a good time. (And whose figure remains mysteriously unafflicted by her many cheese-filled specialties.)

» SERVES 8

1 pound dry elbow macaroni

1 tablespoon olive oil

4 cups shredded sharp
 Cheddar cheese, divided

2 cups shredded Gruyère cheese, divided

1½ cups whole milk

2½ cups half-and-half

½ cup unsalted butter

½ cup all-purpose flour

½ tablespoon kosher salt

½ teaspoon freshly ground black pepper

¼ teaspoon paprika

1. Preheat the oven to 325°F and grease a 9 x 13-inch baking dish.

2. Bring a large pot of salted water to a boil, then pour in the dry macaroni. Cook the pasta for 1 minute less than the package suggests for al dente, then drain the pasta and toss it with the olive oil.

3. Meanwhile, mix the shredded cheeses together and divide the mixture into four 1½-cup amounts. Combine the milk and half-and-half in a medium bowl.

4. Melt the butter in a large saucepan over medium heat, then whisk in the flour until combined. Continue cooking and whisking for 1 minute more. Gradually pour in 2 cups of the milk mixture, whisking constantly, until smooth. Repeat with the remaining 2 cups of the milk mixture.

5. Continue cooking, whisking often, until the sauce has thickened, then remove it from the heat and fold in the salt, pepper, paprika, and 1½ cups of the shredded cheese until melted. Fold in another 1½ cups of the cheese until it has completely melted and the sauce is smooth.

6. In a large bowl, combine the drained pasta with the cheese sauce. Pour half of the cheesy pasta into the prepared baking dish and top it with 1½ cups of the shredded cheese. Repeat with the remaining pasta and remaining 1½ cups of cheese. Bake the dish for 15 minutes, until the cheese is bubbling and beginning to brown.

chapter

4

Family
DINNERS

Even when you live together in a tiny two-room suite, a shared meal can be just what you need to bring the family together. Few things bond people like learning a new skill together while sweating over a hot stove in a borrowed kitchen. (After all, creating such a masterpiece is challenging enough without trying to do so in a kitchenette with little more than a microwave oven.) And there's no need to argue about stolen yogurt when enjoying a home-cooked meal. There is such a thing as too many cooks in the kitchen, though. So carefully choose your cooking companion and allow the others to be pleasantly surprised by a thoroughly edible dinner.

⟫ CHOOSING A RECIPE

When deciding what to dine on as a family, be sure to choose a cherished family recipe like Moira and David do when they select their housekeeper's—no, *Moira's mother's*—enchiladas. No, wait. Actually, choose an *attainable* recipe from anyone's family. Or the internet. Look for recipes with a short list of prepackaged ingredients. Things that come in cans. And unless your cooking partner is the person who perfected the dish, avoid any recipes that make your mouth water at the very thought of them. If you're anything like the Roses, what you're about to do to this recipe will surely tarnish those good memories.

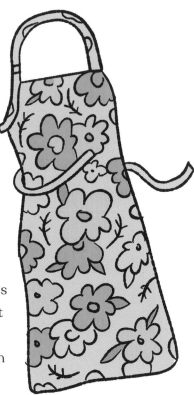

⟫ BEFORE YOU BEGIN

A lot of cooking is about the preparation. Set yourself up for success—or at least for avoiding abject failure—by understanding what you're getting yourself into before you actually get into it. First is making sure the recipe is appropriate for your skill level. If it's not and you choose to move forward anyway (despite a gnawing feeling of impending disaster), then ensure that you have at least a basic understanding of each instruction. And when you realize that you're completely in over your head, just wing it. What's the worst that can happen?

Choose a Helpful Assistant

When preparing a family meal, it can be helpful to have an extra pair of hands in the kitchen. Cooking is a lot for one person. When no one in the room knows how to make so much as a toaster pastry, choose the person most likely to care whether the meal is a complete disaster. You know they'll work hardest to bring the recipe to fruition (and take on the burden of actually cooking the food while you "supervise").

Read Through the Recipe

Learn from David and Moira's mistake: the first time you hear the words "fold in the cheese" should not be when you're elbow deep in an angrily bubbling roux. Read the recipe before you even go near a stove. And not just the ingredients list. The whole thing. (Although you should obviously also read through the ingredients list so you know what you need to buy at the store.) Did you understand all of it? The good news is that if your answer is "no," you still have time to do some research. Or better yet, pick a different recipe.

Do Your Research

Should you both come to an impasse, it can be especially helpful for the assistant to understand how the internet works. Search for terms you don't understand and look for helpful videos of cooking techniques. Depending on how many terms are unfamiliar to you, you may want to carve out some time for this before boiling substances are involved. But it never hurts to learn something new—even if your current meal's fate is already sealed in an oven that smells like burning plastic.

❯ PREPARING THE SPACE

Cooking a real family dinner takes more than a microwave oven and one square foot of counterspace. For something this ambitious, you're going to need to sweet-talk your way into a kitchen with pots and pans. And a working stove. The owner of that kitchen might be a little hesitant about allowing amateur cooks unfettered access to appliances with open flames, but don't take no for an answer. You can do this. (Whether you can do it without covering every surface in bechamel, however, may be asking too much.)

Know Your Limitations

Recreating a beloved meal is a worthy endeavor. And with such delightful results, it can be tempting to schedule such a feat weekly. But there is no shame in leaving meal preparation to the professionals when you realize it's not for you. You're good at many things. You don't have to be good at everything.

Make Room for Genius

Artists need a spotless canvas
and room to work, whether they're
creating detailed masterpieces
or abstract interpretations of the
classics. Demand a clean kitchen that's clear of
tchotchkes, even if the owner of the kitchen is less than cooperative at first.
Following the French technique of *mise en place*, neatly lay out everything
you need so that it's at arm's length and ready to use. Shred the cheese,
slice the vegetables, mix the dry ingredients, and generally have your shit
together before you begin.

Gather Your Tools and Ingredients

Hitch an awkward ride to the grocery store if you have to, but make sure
you have every ingredient on the list before you start in on your recipe.
(The only thing that could be worse than not knowing how to "fold in the
cheese" is not having the fucking cheese.) Then go through your recipe and
see whether your borrowed kitchen has all of the cooking essentials you'll
need to create your meal. If any seem unfamiliar to you, turn to your handy
Wi-Fi-enabled device once again.

❯ ENJOYING THE MEAL

When the cheese has been folded, the meal cooked, and the extras left for
your (thankfully less-than-finicky) kitchen hosts, it's time to enjoy
the fruits of your labor. Set the table with your finest plastic
cups and a wine that can both complement the meal and
conceal its shortcomings. The honor of
the first bite should go to the optimistic
dear whose brilliant idea it was to have
a family dinner. Watch them carefully for
any ill effects before dipping your own
plastic utensil into the dish, and savor a job
reasonably well done!

Mother's Enchiladas

Ready to learn how to feed yourself without raiding someone's yogurt stash like a raccoon? This recipe keeps things simple with plenty of prepackaged ingredients, but keep your phone close just in case!

≫ SERVES 5

1 (10-ounce) can enchilada sauce, divided

4 ounces cream cheese, cubed

1½ cups mild salsa

2 cups shredded cooked chicken

1 (15-ounce) can pinto beans, rinsed and drained

1 (4-ounce) can chopped green chiles

10 (6-inch) flour tortillas

1 cup shredded Mexican-blend cheese

3 tablespoons all-purpose flour

3 tablespoons unsalted butter

2 cups whole milk

2 cups shredded mild cheddar cheese

1. Preheat the oven to 350°F and grease a 9 x 13-inch baking dish. Spread ½ cup of the enchilada sauce over the bottom of the baking dish.

2. In a large saucepan, combine the cream cheese and salsa and cook the mixture over medium heat for 2 to 3 minutes. Then stir in the chicken, beans, and chiles.

3. Spoon about ⅓ cup of the chicken mixture down the center of each tortilla, rolling up the filled tortilla and placing it seam-side down into the prepared baking dish. Once you're finished with all of the tortillas, evenly top them with the remaining enchilada sauce and the Mexican-blend cheese.

4. Make the queso by adding the flour and butter to a large pot over low heat. Cook and whisk them together for 1 to 2 minutes, then continue whisking while you slowly add the milk until you have a thick white sauce.

5. Remove the pot from the heat and use a spatula to gently fold in the cheddar cheese until the mixture is smooth and creamy. (Literally just gently mix the cheese into the sauce by bringing the spatula up from the bottom and over the sauce repeatedly.)

6. Top the enchiladas with the cheese sauce, cover the baking dish with aluminum foil, and bake it until heated through, 25 to 30 minutes. Serve to the surprise and delight of guests with blessedly low expectations.

chapter

5

Games
NIGHTS

Hosting a games night is a lovely opportunity to socialize with acquaintances in a civilized manner with a firm cutoff. (People are a lot.) What games night is not is a party. A proper games night has rules. If you don't want to play by the rules, then games night may not be for you. In fact, let's just go ahead and say the first rule of games night is don't fuck with games night. The evening needs to run a certain way or it won't work. But by choosing the right blend of people and ensuring well-structured game play, you can create a very enjoyable evening for exactly six people. No more, no less. Loneliness might cause panic attacks, but odd numbers and unvetted guests invite chaos.

THE IDEAL GUEST

Everyone knows that you need an even number of people for teams-style game play. But the secret to any successful games night is finding the right kind of player. Think of the people you know who are funny, smart, well-rounded, and have a wide range of knowledge. When you realize that you're the only person who fits that description, lower your expectations. If you should find yourself living in a motel in a boring little town, maybe lower them a little more. You're looking for warm bodies. An *even number* of warm bodies.

EXTENDING INVITATIONS

Although games night is structured, it doesn't require formal invitations. In fact, striking up a conversation with guests before extending a verbal invite works to your advantage. Gauge whether this is a person you really want to spend your evening with. Are they smart? Will they blend well with other guests? Do they get it? If the answer to any of these questions is "no," remember that it's a very small town and you're desperate for human interaction, then swallow your standards and ask them to come anyway. Should you be forced to ask a friend to bring a guest of their choosing, gently remind them that games night is no place for jokes.

ORGANIZING THE EVENING

A well-structured games night requires that game play begin on time. (When you've got a queen bed waiting for you for the first time in months, that schedule needs to be *tight*.) But assuming that people will show up on time is giving the human race far too much credit. Tell guests to arrive at least fifteen minutes before game play is scheduled to begin to give them time to settle into the fraught awkwardness of the evening's events. Tell them game play starts immediately, as well, so they don't fuck up the schedule by arriving even later. If you have everything ready to go when they arrive, you'll know that at least one person in the room has their shit together.

Choose the Games

You want to think *very* carefully before playing an awkward round of Orange Pass with strangers—or worse, with your sister. The few games that have the right vibe for a proper games night include:

- ⚡ Celebrity
- ⚡ Charades
- ⚡ Trivia
- ⚡ Two Truths and a Lie
- ⚡ Cards Against Humanity
- ⚡ Never Have I Ever
- ⚡ Prosecco Pong

Choose no more than three games per evening. And unless you want things to get sloppy (which you don't), no more than one of those should involve alcohol.

Explain the Rules

Explain the rules of the game slowly and clearly to avoid having to repeat yourself more than three times. For especially slow learners, it may be helpful to act out a bit of game play. When you're ready to scream, remind yourself of the panic-attack-inducing loneliness that led to this night. Then laugh at your guests' insipid jokes and answer any inane questions they may have. There *will* be questions, so take Stevie's sage advice and breathe through it.

❯❯ THE GRACIOUS HOST

Cohosting is an actual nightmare and should be avoided at all costs. If you can't avoid it, establish yourself as the dominant host. The junior host can do the glad-handing while you set the strict tone for the evening. Like any magnanimous host, warmly welcome your guests into your domicile (even if those guests were inconsiderate enough to arrive late and endanger your meticulous game-play schedule).

A RARE SOPHISTICATION

Offer Refreshments

To avoid having to eat a guest's mysterious possibly-meat pie, ensure that you have plenty of refreshment alternatives available. You can assume that your guests get enough cheese in their sad little diets, so try to provide crudités or other healthful options. Cocktails are also encouraged but should be enjoyed *after* the initial game setup.

Smooth Things Over

When faced with slim pickings in the personality department, you may find yourself having to fill in conversational gaps. As host, it's your responsibility to ensure that game play runs smoothly. Mentally prepare for the evening with a little "me" time—a good book, coffee with a friend, a small existential crisis. And when your sister inevitably invites dirty strangers into what is effectively your bedroom, avoid giving her the satisfaction of seeing the vein in your eye pop out from indignant fury.

Always Invite an Ally

A good friend can pull you back from the brink of despondency or embarrassment—even if they're also the one who casually pushed you toward it by bringing the worst person they could think of. Should the event turn out to be a complete shit show, you'll know you have one person by your side who gets it.

Be Flexible

The gracious host sets boundaries but remains flexible. Asking your guests not to vomit on your bed, for example, is perfectly reasonable. But when everything inevitably goes to hell because no one is as conscientious (or anal retentive) as you, give up and go with the flow. As the only sober person in the room, at least you know you'll win the games. And isn't that what games night is really about?

How to Play Celebrity

As the host of games night, it's your prerogative to choose the version of game you think best fits the vibe of the evening. With a superior guest list, David's version works beautifully.

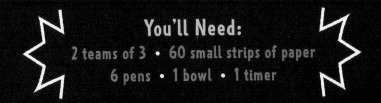

You'll Need:
2 teams of 3 • 60 small strips of paper
6 pens • 1 bowl • 1 timer

GAME SETUP

Have each player write one celebrity's name on each of ten separate pieces of paper, then fold those papers so that no writing is visible and place them in the bowl.

GAME PLAY

1. One player chooses a name from the bowl, opens it without looking at it, and holds it to their forehead (facing out—you're not Johnny Carson).

2. Someone sets the timer for 1 minute. The player's teammates give them hints about their celebrity until they guess it correctly, at which point they pull another piece of paper from the bowl. This continues until the player's time is up.

3. Count the number of celebrities correctly guessed and add that number to the team's overall tally.

4. Repeat with the second team. Game play continues, alternating between different players from each team, until no names are left in the bowl. Whichever team has the most points wins. Obviously.

chapter

6

Girls' Days AND NIGHTS

As Alexis learns (eventually), flying solo isn't all it's cracked up to be. Having your gals by your side can make all the difference when you need to heal a heartbreak, find your way back to yourself, or make a fresh start. You need only give them the chance. That might mean accepting an invitation that initially sounds as appealing as waterboarding, or allowing your own mother to be your wingman. It could also mean letting go of well-laid plans and being open to whatever the evening brings. But it is your solemn duty to take your gals by the hand and lead them to the day of beauty or the night of debauchery they so desperately require. Be their bastion in this bloody skirmish called life!

⟫ A FRIEND IN NEED

Sometimes, it's up to us to notice when a friend could use a little pick-me-up. Whether that calls for a day of indulgence, a night to rock out, or just some time alone, be the magnanimous person who gives it to her. And no matter how much she protests, don't take no for an answer. Poor thing might not realize just how badly she needs a change. And some magic brownies.

Give Her Sage Advice

When, like Alexis, that friend seems a little too desperate for a night out, offer her a sympathetic ear instead. She may need guidance or understanding more than she needs to meet randoms at the local watering hole. Gently guide her to the truth she needs to hear, encourage her fantasies, and offer compliments near her that she can appreciate and internalize. And show her by example that it's perfectly fine to be selfish. Occasionally, of course.

Don't Make Drunken Decisions

Friends often act like a mirror, helping you see the truth. They can also talk you into some of your worst decisions. As Jocelyn learns, the night you've combined magic brownies with yard drinks is not the night to make big moves, like getting a punk-rock haircut. Your hair will grow back. Your dignity, not so much.

Give Her a Break

A friend who, like Moira, has made a hair turban of their silk pajama top and is threatening to stand naked in the road is a friend who is in need of some pampering. Heed her cry for help by treating her to something relaxing, like a manicure or a cocktail. But before you bring her to a one-trick hair stylist, take a moment to put yourself in her shoes. Will she enjoy coming out of the salon looking like a Midwestern nightmare? No? Perhaps the cocktail, then.

⟫ A NIGHT IN

When you're the friend in need, a night of quiet reflection can be just what the doctor (or Twyla) ordered. Indulge in some "me time" with a luxurious face mask and the latest copy of your favorite magazine. (Just because it was published in spring of 1991 doesn't mean it isn't just as relevant today.) Better yet, take this time to better yourself. Cleaning up your room can be the first step in cleaning up your life—and getting your anal-retentive brother off your back.

⟫ A NIGHT OUT

It's important to take time for yourself. But Alexis might say it's also important not to take *too much* time for yourself. You really shouldn't be alone with your thoughts that long. They're not always your friend. Give your brain the night off and let your body take the wheel. In the sense that you put on your best Poison tee or cutest LBD, grab your gals, and hit the town. Not in the sense of trading sexual favors for your freedom, say, in Thailand.

Designate a Driver

It's always wise to designate a driver when cocktails or illegal substances are involved. If there's any risk of the designated driver's being drunker than you by the end of the night, opt for a taxi instead.

For a large girls' trip, you can't do better than a party bus. But, like, an actual party bus. With comfortable leather seats. And a bathroom. Not a sad little school bus that's going to be used to ferry sixth graders to school the next day. (Either way, though, don't forget to take the brownies with you at the end of the night.)

Research the Restaurant

When nights out are scarce, do what you must to make the most of the few you have. Dining cheaply doesn't have to mean eating poorly, and it certainly shouldn't mean enduring a dessert course made with fried chicken like the Jazzagals do. No, thank you. The amateurs among you may need something with grease and carbohydrates to soak up the booze, but you can certainly manage to reserve a table at a more palatable establishment. (Having a large chicken bucket with you on the trip home can't hurt, though.)

Have a Plan B

You know what they say about the best-laid plans of mice and nursing mothers. If your outing goes to shit, don't go crawling back to your newborn bébé. Take the night by the horns and turn it into an even more memorable experience. Take a risk. Play the numbers. Choose a new direction. Every party may have a pooper, but you can leave yours at home with a babysitter in a crop top.

⟫ BE TRUE TO YOU

How the evening unfolds is entirely at your discretion. Looking to meet some randoms? Great. Want to bow out early and wait for the real thing? Totally fine. Need to feel like you're nineteen again and kill some brain cells? Enjoy! Whatever you're in the mood to do, finding like-minded people who will be by your side while you do it can only enhance the experience. And although you may regret some of your choices for the evening, you'll never regret a good time with your gals.

Nanaimo Bars

Nothing could be simpler (or more quintessentially Canadian) than the no-bake Nanaimo bar, a perfectly packable treat for your next girls' night road trip. To avoid provoking a diabetic coma in friends and loved ones, maybe just stick to the one batch. That's already a lot of bars.

≫ MAKES 16 BARS

FOR THE BOTTOM LAYER
½ cup unsalted butter, softened
¼ cup granulated sugar
5 tablespoons unsweetened cocoa powder
1 large egg, beaten
1¾ cups graham cracker crumbs
1 cup flaked coconut
½ cup finely chopped almonds

FOR THE MIDDLE LAYER
½ cup unsalted butter, softened
3 tablespoons heavy cream
2 tablespoons custard powder
2 cups confectioners' sugar

FOR THE TOP LAYER
4 (1-ounce) squares semisweet
    baking chocolate
2 teaspoons unsalted butter

1. To make the bottom layer, combine the butter, granulated sugar, and cocoa powder in the top of a double boiler over medium-low heat. (Just Google it.) Cook, stirring frequently, until the mixture is melted and smooth, about 2 minutes. Stir in the egg until the mixture thickens, 2 to 3 minutes more. Remove the bowl from the heat and stir in the graham cracker crumbs, coconut flakes, and almonds. Press the mixture into the bottom of an ungreased 8 x 8-inch pan.

2. To make the middle layer, use a hand or stand mixer on medium speed to cream together the butter, heavy cream, and custard powder until the mixture is light and fluffy. Slowly mix in the confectioners' sugar until smooth, then spread the mixture evenly over the bottom layer in the pan. Transfer the pan to the refrigerator to chill until set, about 1 hour.

3. Meanwhile, prepare the top layer. Add the semisweet chocolate and butter to a small microwavable bowl and heat in 30-second increments, stirring in between, just until combined and smooth.

4. Spread the chocolate mixture over the chilled bars and restrain yourself long enough to let it set completely before cutting into squares and serving.

chapter

7

Sales SCHEMES

When you hit rock bottom, you may find a box of unsellable skincare or essential oils waiting there for you. After all, multilevel marketing schemes (MLMs), much like cults, prey on the weak and vulnerable. But desperate times call for desperate motel-room sales pitches to those you can only hope are weaker and more vulnerable than you. Or for throwing yourself into your work while you turn a blind eye to red flags that should be growing more glaring by the minute. Although a person of sound mind who's in a good place in their life might conclude that MLMs are beneath them, there is no shame in hoping for better things to come. Like a Champagne Audi.

KNOW WHAT YOU'RE SELLING

Before you can talk unwitting friends and acquaintances into being the next brick in your pyramid, you'll need to have at least a vague understanding of what you're selling. Is it a skincare product? A lifestyle? A front-row ticket to the rapture? Watch the marketing video and take notes, or attend a class yourself before inviting others. Just don't think too hard about what you're hearing if you want to be able to sell the thing with a clear conscience.

SELLING A PRODUCT

Judging by Jocelyn's home, the residents of Schitt's Creek were no strangers to a Tupperware party long before a certain cosmetics company rolled into town. What that tells you is that your multilevel marketing scheme can work . . . as long as it hasn't already made executive area managers of half the fucking town. All you need is the right product and an enticing sales pitch. And probably some cheese. Lots of cheese.

Keep It Classy

Regardless of what product you're selling and whether it has the market value of a drugstore lip balm, you'll want to offer an upscale sales environment. A luncheon with elegant hors d'oeuvres is just what the plastic surgeon ordered for a skincare launch. And when that proves impossible (because, let's face it, you wouldn't be hawking this crap if you had the money for canapés), you can quickly and inexpensively procure crackers, cheese, and salami from the general store.

SUNLESS BRONZER

Gauge Interest

Rather than surprising guests with your (extremely well-acted) sales pitch, do a little reconnaissance work ahead of time. You would be shocked by how many may have been

~~suckered into~~ influenced by a similar pitch. And you don't want that shock to come mid-pitch. As David and Moira learn, you only think you've hit rock bottom until you've tried to sell garbage cosmetics to townies only to discover they rank higher than you do in the company. Save yourself the time, frustration, and Champagne-like beverages and get to know your ~~marks~~ customers before you pop that cork.

CHOOSE THE RIGHT BUSINESS PARTNER

No matter what kind of scheme you're running, it's important to trust only the shrewdest of associates with your plan—especially where money is involved. For example, you wouldn't ask someone like Alexis, who doesn't know the difference between a pint and a 10-gallon can, to buy black-market milk for you. That would be foolish. Or someone like Roland, who would crack under the pressure of a paper clip and at the worst possible time. In fact, it might be wiser to follow that old adage: "If you want it done right, do it yourself."

SELLING A LIFESTYLE

There's very little difference between selling a product and selling a lifestyle. Either way, you should have at least a basic understanding of what you're selling before getting into bed with a company (and possibly their super-hot-however-stupidly-named spokesman). Talk to employees and members alike to get a clear picture of the company's principles and systems. And if you're unable to find any of the organization's former members because they've gone through "the Gateway," consider taking a closer look before putting your friends in danger. Or just run in the opposite direction. Yeah, probably that.

Be Ready to Change Tack

Whether you've just discovered that your entire town is higher on the pyramid than you are or that you're working on brand awareness for a cult, you may find yourself in need of a hard out. Practice your "gotcha" face before beginning any pitch, and keep your eyes peeled for emergency exits at all times.

Clarify That Language

Alexis would tell you that it's best to take a beat and ask some questions when the higher-ups are being super vague and sketchy about a program that you're selling to your friends. Like, why did you have to change out of exercise clothes and into a tunic? Why is your exercise instructor named after a class of fruit? And is he using motivational language or code for science-fiction-level end-times events? Friends don't let friends join a cult, even if they're just being supportive.

Peek at the Merch

One way to tell how deep the rabbit hole goes in your new business venture is to look at the marketing materials it uses. Crystal water may seem innocuous enough, but tapes that have to be played at a certain speed while you sleep? That might be a red flag. Like, a blood-red flag. Like a blood-red flag that's on fire. And if your most gullible friend saw the duvet-size flag and you didn't, maybe you need some time to reflect before jumping into your *next* business venture.

Make Sure Everyone's Comfortable

Sometimes you miss the blaring warning sirens, and that's okay. But if one of your friends is acting like a dog in Pompeii, take note. Sure, that friend—like Stevie—might habitually point out the flaws of, well, every single thing and person they encounter throughout every day of their life. Just because that's their personality doesn't make them wrong. Take their questions to the higher-ups and you might have just enough time to ditch the tunics and hit the road before you're shoved through the Gateway.

Energizing Harvest Smoothie (for Ascending)

You'll need to keep your energy up if you want to ascend, and that's easier said than done when you've just spent an hour on a stair-climber. A few sips of this smoothie will perk you right up—and without any unfortunate side effects.

» SERVES 2 TO 4

2 cups fresh spinach

2 cups water

1 cup frozen mango chunks

1 cup frozen pineapple chunks

2 large bananas, sliced

2 tablespoons chia seeds

1. In a high-speed blender, blend the spinach and water together until smooth. Add the mango, pineapple, bananas, and chia seeds and blend until smooth again.

2. Enjoy! (Seriously. That's it. It's not rocket science.)

chapter

8

Mystery NIGHTS

Done correctly, the humble theme party can be the event of the year. Done poorly, however, the experience will have people avoiding your gaze when the event's anniversary nears. Add to that the pressure of planning a murder on top of planning your party, and pulling off this event becomes something of a Herculean task. You'll need thoughtful party favors, top-notch catering, a signature cocktail, and theme-appropriate music and decorations as well as a murderer who will both show up at the party and avoid committing any real crimes. Creating such an elaborate experience isn't for everyone, so don't be afraid to seek counsel from an experienced party planner if you find yourself in over your head.

CHOOSING A THEME

You might be thinking, "Isn't the theme of my murder mystery party a murder mystery?" No dear, it's not. Your theme *encompasses* the murder mystery, giving it context. Will your party be Agatha Christie–themed and feature your very own Hercule Poirot? Will it be Roaring Twenties–themed, giving you an occasion to wear that cute little flapper dress you rocked at Leo's birthday bash? As the host, you get to choose whatever strikes your fancy! (And fits within your budget, since you won't be charging anyone for the pleasure of attending.)

GETTING THOSE RSVPS

As Twyla learns year after year, murder mysteries hinge on all of the key players actually attending the party, which is why it's crucial to manage your guest list. Get firm RSVPs well in advance. *Firm.* Do not allow anyone to hem and haw until there are mere hours left with which to plan their part in the evening, from bringer of bagel bites to covert killer. Luckily, there are things you can do as host to encourage enthusiasm and affirmative responses from guests.

Offer Catering

Requiring guests to bring from their own home a slow cooker full of pot roast or an heirloom platter lined with crudités is the quickest way to elicit a "no" from world-weary invitees. As the host of any gathering, you assume the responsibility for feeding your guests. Moira's suggestion of Wagyu sliders may be too ambitious for a small-town event, but you could certainly offer a selection of goods from the local café . . . especially if you work at the local café. You can nevertheless embolden guests to bring the odd treat or bottle, though. There is still such a thing as a hostess gift.

Start with Your VIPs

You might be foolishly tempted to start your guest list with your dearest friends, but that is not how you fill a room. Begin your list instead with the guests who have the most pull among the other people in the town. For those select few, sweeten the offer. Perhaps a cocktail in their name or an extra party favor might tempt them. Bag the right VIP and the rest will fall like dominoes in a line all the way to your doorstep on the night of the event.

Playing the Game

While you plan your elaborate murder mystery event, you may need to play a little game of your own to get more disillusioned guests to attend. Your past limitations as a host may be coming back to haunt you. Exorcise them by talking up the changes you've made to this year's event. And if that doesn't work, don't be afraid to use your wiles. A little flattery can go a long way when persuading a local tastemaker to help you grow your guest list.

Invite Trustworthy Guests

Keep a watchful eye on the guest list, ensuring that you know the name and criminal history of any plus-ones. A murder mystery party is no place for actual criminals. Between the booze and the game, it would be far too easy for a shifty character to make off with every gold watch in the room.

COMMITTING A (FICTITIOUS) MURDER

Once you have a handle on the event details, you can turn your attention to the needs of the game itself. Planning a murder mystery requires careful coordination of characters, props, and timing. Not to mention making sure the murderer is on hand throughout the evening. Should you drop any one of these balls, this may be the last event of yours that any guests attend. Take at least as much time to plot out the details of the game as you do to select your signature cocktail.

Choose Your Murderer Carefully

Like Twyla, you might want to bestow the honor of the biggest part—the murderer—on the person who's been most helpful in making your party a success. But take a moment to think. Did you actually hear the would-be murderer RSVP for the full evening? Does this person have a habit of following through on promises? Whoever you choose to be your cold-blooded killer should have enough humanity to both show up to your party and stay for the duration of it. Just in case, have a backup assassin on hand.

Hand Out Assignments

Character roles should be assigned well in advance of the party so that you're able to easily hand out props and clues according to the game's schedule. Only assign roles to those who have offered a firm "yes" in response to your invitation, lest you have to act out multiple parts yourself like you're starring in a sad one-woman play. And for fuck's sake, write it all down. No one wants to be stuck in murder-mystery hell trying to guess the name of a killer who doesn't exist because you forgot to assign the role.

Get Out Alive

Unless you want your party and your social standing to die alongside your murder victim, make sure you keep the refreshments flowing and the evening moving along at a good clip. No sane adult wants to be at a party until 3 a.m. Taking into account the game play, catering, and general merriment, the party should last no more than three hours and have a cutoff time as firm as that RSVP list. As Moira might advise, it's always best to leave people wanting more.

Crime of Passion

No event would be complete without a signature cocktail, much less an event that requires audience participation. This vodka-based beauty is as sunny and sweet as Twyla herself and as fruity as her signature smoothie (on the days that it's more fruity than earthy).

» SERVES 1

Ice cubes
½ teaspoon grapefruit zest
1½ ounces passionfruit vodka
½ ounce plum wine
½ ounce lime juice
1 teaspoon simple syrup
1 slice grapefruit, for garnish

1. Fill a rocks glass and a shaker with ice.

2. Add all of the ingredients to the shaker (except for the garnish, obviously). Shake until cold, then strain the cocktail into the glass and garnish with the slice of grapefruit.

chapter

9

House PARTIES

Once you find a place to call your own, it's only natural to want to invite friends over to enjoy the space with you. And help you furnish it with expensive gifts. If you do choose to relive the carefree glory days of your high school experience with a raucous house party, you are also choosing to forgo gifts. So, consider that. But if Ray were popping into *your* rented room every five minutes, you'd probably want to throw a rager in your new apartment, too. Take it from Patrick—nothing says, "I'm a fully functional adult with my own business and a studio apartment" like a matching pajama set and multicolored party shots. Maybe learn from his mistakes, too, and skip any potentially inflammatory games.

≫ HOUSEWARMING VS. HOUSE PARTY

When you move into a new house or apartment, have finally unpacked the boxes, and have everything just the way you want it, your first instinct is probably *not* to fill that space with sloppy drunks and Solo cups. *That* is a house party, and it's strictly for frat boys and high schoolers who've stolen the key to their parents' liquor cabinet. A house*warming*, however, is an elegant affair involving a limited number of people, civilized conversation, and a very good bottle of Merlot. If you're over the age of thirty, a house party is not a good look for you.

≫ CHOOSING A THEME

Should you choose to ignore the fact that you're over thirty—and of course you will—you'll need a theme for your house party. Opt for one that's creative yet relatable, to get people excited about attending, and not something that requires enough advance notice to order handcrafted accessories from Italy. And here's the important note: Imagine all the problems that theme can cause before finalizing it. Throwbacks are fun, but it might be wiser to elevate the party to your current age rather than trying to rewrite your past.

Set a Dress Code

Choosing a theme with a lot of room for interpretation can have some unintended consequences, like *your* boyfriend (and half the party, honestly) lusting after your sister's boyfriend. Without policing your guests' bodies, offer suggestions for party-appropriate attire. Should you prefer not to feel like you have unwittingly hosted a nudist event or an afterparty at Fyre Festival, remind your guests that hypothermia is real and encourage more sophisticated apparel.

Preselect the Games

Your theme should also inform which games you choose to play with your guests. A housewarming, with its intimate guest list of well-adjusted adults, might benefit from an ice-breaking game of Charades. The likes of Never Have I Ever, Spin the Bottle, Twister, and Truth or Dare, however, suit a drunken house party perfectly. Whatever you do, don't let people suggest games on the fly. These things need structure. See "Games Night" (page 29) for ground rules that will ensure there's no sloppy game play resulting in hurt feelings or sibling drama.

Prepare Refreshments

Much like the games, your refreshments should complement the theme of the night. Gin-based drinks in cocktail glasses would work beautifully for a "Roaring Twenties" theme. A trio of wines served with a lovely cheeseboard of Brie and tapenade would do well for a quiet night. And of course, beer, chips, and party shots are standard fare for a high school party. (Which you would obviously know. Because of all the high school parties you attended.) The most important thing is that there are enough snacks to soak up all the alcohol.

❯❯ AVOIDING DRAMA

Depending on the night's theme, a self-serve bar could be a very dangerous party feature. Learn from Patrick's mistake and monitor guests who seem like they've overindulged. Offer them water or coffee in place of yet another cup of 100-proof mystery punch. You wouldn't want to impede anyone's good time, of course. But a sloppy drunk is not going to be a good time for you. Avoid drama by allowing the alcohol to mysteriously disappear at a predetermined interval. And by keeping established couples out of any spin-the-bottle situations. It's for the best.

⟫ POST-PARTY CLEANUP

Once you've hit a natural stopping point (or your predetermined cutoff point) for the evening, convey your gratitude to your guests for coming—and for leaving. Make sure that any particularly troublesome tsetse-fly–like guests find the door. Then do a quick search of the space for partygoers who've passed out in odd places. With the party finished, you can finally enjoy some peace and quiet in your new home. While you disinfect every surface.

Take Out the Trash

The trouble with hosting any sort of housewarming party is that you're left holding the trash bags at the end of the night. You certainly can't go to sleep in your new home with party and relationship detritus lying around. And God knows that not a single guest will stay to help you clean. Not that you would want them to. You want guests to leave having enjoyed themselves, but you also want the people who created this mess to get the fuck out. Plus, you'd have to supervise them, and that's just a waste of energy you don't have.

Warn Guests Against Pregaming

There's absolutely no need for guests to pregame before attending a housewarming—this isn't Burning Man. Let friends know that there will be plenty of drink options and opportunities at the party. And that no one is crashing on your floor at the end of the night, so they better rein that shit in.

Clear the Air

At the end of the night, light a few candles to freshen up your space. And maybe an herb bundle to cleanse drunken stupidity from your new home. Just make sure you blow everything out before going to bed. You *just* got that renters' insurance. (By the way, get renters' insurance.) While you're at it, clarify any misunderstandings or hurt feelings that may have cropped up throughout the evening. You want to nestle into your new bed with a clean apartment and a clear head.

Party Shots

With no salad bowl full of E in sight, you'll have to settle for this old standard. Luckily, these Party Shots are delicious. The key is to use those tiny plastic cups that allow you to push the gelatin into your mouth. (You know, the ones they gave you for ketchup at the food court in the mall. Back in high school.)

≫ MAKES 16 SHOTS

½ cup cold water
½ cup vodka or other liquor
1 (3-ounce) package gelatin, any flavor
1 cup boiling water

1. In a small bowl, combine the cold water and liquor. Place the mixture in the refrigerator to chill.

2. Meanwhile, add the gelatin to another small bowl and slowly (and carefully) pour in the boiling water. Stir the two together until the gelatin has completely dissolved.

3. Pour the gelatin mixture into the cooled liquor mixture and stir well before pouring the finished gelatin into 16 tiny cups.

4. Refrigerate the party shots until set, at least 2 hours but preferably overnight.

5. Repeat these steps with different flavors to create multiple flavor options, and try not to consume them all before the partygoers arrive.

chapter

10

Romantic PICNICS

Enjoying your partner's company on a beautiful summer day over good cheese? That can be everything you need to celebrate life, rekindle romance, and mark a new beginning. Don't be fooled by the simple pleasures of a picnic, though. Even this humble al fresco event requires a little forethought and care if you want it to end with a passionate embrace and not a citation for indecent exposure. From making a plan and letting your partner in on it, to wearing the right pants and keeping them on, you have plenty of details to consider. But the most important thing is to appreciate and enjoy this time you have together. (You might just have to lower your expectations a smidgen to do it.)

PREPARING YOUR PARTNER

Surprising your loved one with a romantic excursion is an incredibly thoughtful and well-intentioned gesture. But as Patrick learns, the road to hell is paved with the good intentions of the partners of high-maintenance people. Understand first just exactly who it is you're taking on this picnic. Are they a nature person? A fan of impulsive mountain hikes? Or would they, like David, really prefer dining outside at the café or reenacting scenes from their favorite romantic comedies? Plan accordingly.

Set Expectations

Spontaneity has its place, and it's not on a fucking hiking trail. An activity like hiking requires things like thick-soled boots, the right clothing, bug spray, and a first-aid kit. If you don't give your partner a heads-up about your plans, they might show up in a heavy black sweater and high-tops with nary a bandage in sight. And if you trick your partner into going on a hike when they think they'll be sitting on a park bench, you'll have only yourself to blame for the passive-aggressive sniping that ensues.

Dress Appropriately

Donning your own hiking gear in preparation for your picnic should be your first clue that it's important to dress appropriately. Sweaters and high-tops might keep the ticks at bay on a long midsummer hike, but they won't do anything for your picnic partner's disposition. Give them the opportunity to grab some gear of their own, and you might actually get to enjoy this picnic. (Although there's a very real chance that, no matter what your partner wears, they may not be thrilled with having to earn their cheese through actual physical activity.)

Keep Your Clothes On

Take it from Mr. Rose: treating a public park like your own personal Grecian bath has some very obvious consequences, like police officers having to literally fish you out of an algae-filled creek. Those are not the mineral waters of Evian, and there are worse things than losing a truly stupidly expensive watch. (Okay, maybe there aren't. If you could put a price on pride, it would almost certainly be less than $100,000.) Skip the skinny-dipping on public property and enjoy your picnic on dry land, fully clothed—for the benefit of both your skin and everyone else's eyes.

PACKING YOUR BASKET (OR BACKPACK)

One might think that packing a picnic basket is a task so simple that even Roland could do it. (Picnics do tend to be cheese-centric, after all.) And if you're not traveling far, a simple blanket for spreading across lush grass and a well-stocked picnic basket are more than enough for a lovely afternoon. But should you have more ambitious plans for the day, you'll need to pack those bags just as thoughtfully as you would carry-on luggage for a three-day trip to Mykonos.

Safety First

It may not seem like it, but a first-aid kit is actually *more* important than Champagne. (You should definitely bring an extra bag if you need to in order to pack both, though.) If you don't have room for a full kit, at least pack some hand sanitizer and bandages. That should be enough for most emergencies, like a minor foot injury or major foot-in-mouth issues. For your own personal safety on a long hike, you should also pack some accessible snacks to tide your partner over until you reach that romantic overlook.

Match the Food to the Effort

No one wants to hike a mile in a furry sweater with a heavy bag on their back just for some cheese. (Okay, it is a pretty good motivator. But it also requires bulky insulation to survive the trek, so it's really a draw.) Make sure you pack enough food to satisfy the appetite you'll work up while winding your way through the woods . . . and enduring an existential crisis about having to wind your way through the woods just to get some cheese. You're not a fucking mouse. There had better be some tapenade to go with that Brie.

Leave the Phone on Silent

Don't ruin a lovely afternoon with shop talk or online bidding wars. It may go against your every instinct to keep your phone out of your hand, but it will do you no good to look back on a volatile career or down on a long, beautiful hike. Unless, of course, the looking down helps you avoid thorn-filled branches.

Consider Your Comfort

For lack of a park bench and the lap of a loving husband, you'll need to pack some small comforts in your picnic basket. A soft yet sturdy blanket is a must—one that adds a little luxury while also putting a good, thick barrier between you and any dirt. Another helpful accessory is an umbrella. Carrying a simple parasol can increase your comfort, save you from harmful UV rays, and (as Moira demonstrates) perfectly complement your outfit all at the same time.

⟫ LIVE IN THE MOMENT

There's nothing quite like a near-death experience or a life-changing event to make you thankful for each day you have with a loved one. Take a moment to truly appreciate your partner. (Like, verbally. Out loud. They need it.) And savor this time you have together, even if it means pretending to be grateful for unprompted physical activity or taking a risk in a public creek. You could be killed by a toaster fire tomorrow, so enjoy today!

Cheeseball for Lovers

Take a page out of Roland and Jocelyn's book and whip up this artery-clogging aphrodisiac the next time you're feeling romantic. Just be sure to serve it with a spreading knife to avoid crumbling crackers ruining its sensual effect.

» SERVES 24

16 ounces cream cheese, softened

2 cups freshly grated sharp cheddar cheese

2 medium green onions, chopped

1 teaspoon Worcestershire sauce

1 teaspoon hot pepper sauce

1 teaspoon dried parsley flakes

½ teaspoon garlic powder

½ teaspoon dried oregano

Dash of freshly ground black pepper

⅔ cup pecans, finely chopped

1. Add the cream cheese to a mixing bowl and stir until smooth. Then stir in the grated cheese, green onion, sauces, and spices until well combined and creamy.

2. Using a spatula, scrape the cheese mixture into the center of the bowl. Then use your lightly greased hands to mold it into a ball.

3. Wrap the cheeseball tightly in plastic wrap and refrigerate it for 20 to 30 minutes to set.

4. Pour the chopped pecans onto a plate. Gently roll and press the cheeseball into the pecans until the ball is completely coated, scooping up more pecans and pressing them into the cheese as needed.

5. Re-cover the cheeseball in plastic wrap and refrigerate it for about 1 hour to set completely. Allow it to thaw and soften slightly before serving with crackers, about 20 minutes. (Or freeze the damn thing and skip the ice pack on your hike. It should soften by the time you make it to the overlook.)

chapter

11

Baby SHOWERS

A baby shower is an age-old tradition of showering an expecting mommy with gifts to help her prepare for the baby's arrival. It's a really lovely way for a community to come together in the spirit of "it takes a village." But someone still has to plan and pay for it. If that someone is you, take a deep breath and light a patchouli candle to calm your chi. A baby shower is unlike any event you've planned before. Nonsensical food restrictions, disgusting games, and truly ugly decorations are just a few of the obstacles you'll face on this particular journey. In order to turn this event into something that non-pregnant people actually want to attend and enjoy, you may need to get a little creative.

SHOWERING VS. SPRINKLING

When the mommy-to-be already has one baby under her belt and presumably a full shower to go with it, she may only need a sprinkling of baby-related accoutrements. That's where a "baby sprinkle" comes in. Of course, that doesn't really apply when Mommy's last baby was born three full decades previously. That cobweb-covered crib in her attic was surely recalled a good twenty-nine years ago, and Baby doesn't want to be seen in bell-bottoms. So you're going to want to go with the full shower on that one.

BEING A GOOD FRIEND

When your pregnant friend . . . or loose acquaintance . . . walks up to you looking like Chewbacca in a floral robe, talking about throwing her own baby shower, do as David does and take a hint. A generous person would now offer to plan her shower for her. Bear in mind that doing so means putting the needs and desires of the mommy-to-be ahead of your own. Even if that means attending a party without alcohol. On the other hand, people who enjoy alcohol will outnumber people who are pregnant, so what would Emily Post have to say about ignoring *their* needs and desires?

Expand the Guest List

Men aren't traditionally invited to baby showers and sprinkles, but in a small town with limited gifting options, you take all the gift-giving guests you can squeeze into a living room. Just don't let Daddy have any say in the planning unless you want to poison or traumatize your guests. As host, it's your name and reputation on the line here.

Keep Mommy in Mind

Unlike most events that feature an honoree, baby showers are typically not planned around the host's desires, the sponsor's brand, or even the guests' pleasure. This is for Mommy and Mommy alone. So, if Mommy wants streamers and balloons, bid adieu to any fantasies you have about elegant drapings and delicious soft cheeses. Unless you've already bought the cheese and planned a charcuterie table around it.

Then that can be Mommy's gift to her friends for enduring an evening of inane baby-themed games. As Jocelyn would probably tell you, beggars can't be choosers.

Set a Budget

Considering that the point of a shower is to give the new mom a financial head start, it wouldn't make much sense for her to go into hock for it. The friend/unwilling event planner throwing the shower pays for the shower. Keep that in mind when setting the budget. After all, you wouldn't want your friend feeling beholden to you for flying in expensive cuts of fish. That doesn't mean, though, that you can't endeavor to rise above the very low bar of dollar-store decorations.

Organize the Entertainment

Just because the event is celebrating a new baby does not mean that the games you play have to be geared toward children. Only a simpleminded first-grader would stick their nose in diapers filled with unidentified substances. (It could be *cheap* chocolate. Ew.) Another popular game for showers is the Clothespin Game, where you avoid saying the word "baby" to keep your clothespin. Obviously, this will come more naturally to those who, like David, generally avoid saying the word "baby" at all. Whichever game you choose, avoid throwing things at the mommy-to-be. It lacks a certain sophistication.

❯ TRADITIONAL CONSIDERATIONS

Once you have a basic understanding of the requirements of a baby shower, you can set about planning it. But not before then. You don't want to have to talk your fishmonger into accepting a return of the branzino you ordered. Although, what's done is done. It's not like the mommy-to-be needs to eat the fish. She can probably eat the crudités. And, really, she knew what she was getting into when she asked you to plan this thing.

Choosing a Venue

Ideally, you would host a friend's baby shower in a well-appointed restaurant, perhaps over tea and lovely little French pastries. When you don't get a say in choosing the venue, however, you have to make do with what you're given. With some well-designed charcuterie and upscale decorations, you can make any space work for you. Even spaces that smell like cheese and look like they haven't been updated in decades.

Decorating the Space

When decorating someone's home, it's even more important that you elevate the space. This is a gathering for adults, whose tastes have hopefully evolved beyond potato chips and balloons. Movie posters, baby-shaped piñatas, pastel-colored streamers, and anything else you might find at a five-year-old's birthday party are also out. Think: cohesive color scheme, a variety of food stations, and a dedicated gift area. The goal here is to make you forget you're in Mommy's living room entirely.

Furnishing Refreshments

You may not be aware of this, but doctors actually recommend that pregnant women avoid certain fish, soft cheeses, cold cuts, and even wine. In other words, everything you would want at a party. But baby showers are for the mommy-to-be, so everyone else in attendance will just have to suck it up. Except at your party, because this mommy-to-be gave you creative control. Besides, branzino is low in mercury. (But it's also low in flavor for a ridiculously expensive fish, so maybe cancel that order and opt for some brisket from the café instead.)

How to Play the Diaper Game

If your guest of honor insists on playing this disgusting game instead of crowd-favorite Sleepy Mommy, you can at least make the best of it by using quality organic chocolates. But under no circumstances are guests to do anything except *smell* the chocolate.

You'll Need

Marker • 5 (clean) disposable diapers
5 different kinds of fun-size candy bars
Paper • Pens

GAME SETUP

Use a marker to number the diapers on the outside. Open the candies and put one in the center of each diaper, then microwave the diapers for 20 seconds each to melt the chocolate. Once melted, squish the chocolate further into the diaper, then leave the diapers open. Give everyone a piece of paper and a pen.

GAME PLAY

1. Each diaper gets passed around from player to player so that they can smell (and only smell) the contents.

2. Players write down the diaper number and their guess as to what variety of candy bar was inside on a piece of paper. They do not say their guess aloud.

3. Whoever has the most correct answers wins a prize. That's it. (You're sniffing diapers. It's not *Jeopardy!*.)

chapter

12

Birthday PARTIES

Birthday parties may be some of the most stressful events to plan because they're some of the most personal. You want this party to be everything your loved one could hope for. That's a lot of pressure. And when your loved one tells you that they've always wanted a surprise party, pity quickly turns to panic. You'll need to keep that secret locked up better than Alexis in a Saudi palace. Reaching out to friends and family for help can take some of the burden off your shoulders. Or make it heavier. It really depends on the friends and family you reach out to, doesn't it? Either way, birthday parties take time, planning, and a *que será, será* attitude that few party planners possess. So good luck with that.

❯❯ THE PERILS OF SURPRISE PARTIES

However well intentioned, a surprise party in the wrong hands can be just the kind of sad, tacky event that pushes a person to avoid their birthday entirely. Done well, a surprise party can be the best night of a person's life. But it takes a lot to do a surprise party well, like good taste and friends who can keep a fucking secret. Although daunting to plan, surprise parties really are one of the most memorable ways to celebrate a loved one's birthday.

❯❯ KEEPING THE SECRET

If you want the tears of genuine surprise and heartfelt gratitude, you need to keep your party planning under wraps. Of course, as David demonstrates twice, that's easier said than done. The minute you tell other people what you're planning, you risk the entire operation. That's why it's really best to wait until the last possible second to let people in on the surprise. Really. Minutes before the party, if you can. It'll be like a fun surprise for everyone. And obviously you have to try to get through the day without giving up the goods yourself.

Come Up with a Cover Story

Take more than a few moments to craft your cover story. The lie you tell your loved one—and, therefore, ask others to tell them—has to be bulletproof. It has to be simple enough that even an amiable moron (like Roland) can keep it straight and interesting enough to entice your intended target. But that's where things get tricky. The last thing you need is your loved one rolling up their sleeves to help with the decoy event or thinking that your venue is a virus-laden cesspool (Twyla's right—cover stories involving health-code violations should be avoided).

Know Who to Trust

Trusting only a select few with the truth is your best hope at pulling off your surprise, but it's not without risk. Of your friends, ask yourself, who can keep a secret? Who can keep a cover story straight? Who can act (at least well enough to star in a community theater production)? If there's no overlap in those answers, you have a problem. How would you feel about planning the entire party yourself and surprising everyone in attendance, including the honoree? Yeah, no, that would be a lot. Choose the friend who can keep a secret.

Keep Surprise Guests Separate

Adding surprise guests to the mix is just asking for the kind of excitement and confusion that leads to loose lips. If you don't want anyone spilling any beans, it's best to keep surprise guests hidden away until the very last minute. Maybe learn from David's mistake with Patrick's parents and give those guests special instructions not to speak to anyone until the party. Or at least until they speak to you. You never know who's keeping secrets completely unrelated to the festivities, and these things can unravel very quickly.

❯ HAVE ALL THE FACTS

When planning a surprise party for someone else, it's likely that you won't know some guests as well as you know others. And there's nothing wrong with that. But it's a good idea to do a little covert information gathering while making up the guest list. Knowing whether anyone's had a spat or whether your loved one's parents are fully informed can help you make decisions about the party. When you fail to have all the facts, follow David's lead—a luxurious gift basket can be a lovely way to say, "Sorry, I fucked up."

❯ DEAL WITH THE DETAILS

The element of surprise will consume most of your waking thoughts until you flip those lights on and scare the bejesus out of your unwitting loved one. But there are other details to consider when planning a birthday party, like where you'll hold it, how you'll decorate it, and what you'll serve at it. Just little things, really. What matters most is that the honoree enjoys their night, and that only depends on who's there to celebrate it with them. Or to celebrate *them*, if you're Moira.

Ask for Help

One of the great things about a small town is how willing everyone is to lend a hand. If you're already asking people to help you pull off an elaborate ruse, you may as well ask them for help with setup, too. Someone might even have candles to lend you so that you don't end up doing community service for petty theft.

Find a Venue

Choosing the right venue for your party depends on how many guests you've invited, where your loved one feels most comfortable, and whether you have access to or money for a proper venue. When you're tight on time and funds, work with what you've got. With the right decor, you can transform a rustic barn or a sweet little café into an elegant event space. Do a last site survey the day of the party to ensure that there's adjustable lighting for the initial surprise and plenty of room for dancing.

Work within Your Budget

When you're on a shoestring budget, you just need to get creative. The same colorful paper cups you'll use for beverages can become lovely lanterns when strung onto strands of globe lights, and local flowers can make beautiful accents in painted Mason jars. Spend your money on one really great surprise, like a decadent cake, and avoid over-ordering specialty foods that cost a small fortune. No one wants you chasing them around with uneaten crab cakes all night.

Chocolate Ganache Torte Cake

Decorations and crustacean hand pies are all well and good, but the cake makes the party. This isn't the time for your vanilla buttercream. This is the time for rich, chocolaty, indulgent ganache. Make your own rather than special ordering one and you may even have enough money for candles!

⟫ SERVES 10 TO 12

FOR THE CAKE
½ cup (1 stick) unsalted butter, softened
1 cup sugar
4 extra-large eggs, at room temperature
1⅓ cups chocolate syrup
1 tablespoon pure vanilla extract
1 cup all-purpose flour

FOR THE GANACHE
½ cup heavy cream
8 ounces good-quality
   semisweet chocolate chips
1 teaspoon instant coffee

1. Preheat the oven to 325°F. Butter an 8-inch round cake pan, line it with parchment paper, then butter and flour the bottom and sides of the pan (including the paper).

2. To make the cake, in the bowl of a stand mixer fitted with a paddle attachment, cream together the butter and sugar until light and fluffy. Continue mixing while adding the eggs one at a time. Then mix in the chocolate syrup and vanilla. When that's incorporated and smooth, gradually add the flour and mix until just combined.

3. Pour the finished batter into the pan and bake for 40 to 45 minutes, or until just set in the middle and a toothpick inserted into the center comes out clean. Remove the cake from the oven and let it cool in the pan.

4. To make the ganache, add the heavy cream, chocolate chips, and instant coffee to a heatproof bowl over simmering water (a double boiler) and stir until smooth and warm.

5. Turn the cake out onto a wire rack and smooth the ganache over the top of it, either stopping at the edges or covering the sides as well, before serving it.

chapter

13

Anniversary
DINNERS

DINNER COUPON

4 FOR 3

If the Rose family's story has taught you anything, it's
that you shouldn't take a single day of fortune for granted,
and that includes those days you are fortunate in love.
Never miss an opportunity to celebrate your relationship's
surviving yet another intrepid voyage around the sun.
Whether you're basically penniless and stuck in a Podunk
town or you're thousands of miles apart, there are plenty
of ways to mark the occasion. Even a grand gesture
can be simple to pull off if you know the right people.
The most important thing is that you celebrate the day
together. And perhaps with a few friends. Or frenemies. But
preferably alone. Together.

KNOW YOUR PARTNER'S EXPECTATIONS

When you've been with your partner long enough to celebrate an anniversary, you should have some inkling as to their expectations for the day. Will they be satisfied with a sad breakfast cupcake? Or will they, like Moira, be expecting a trail of breakfast cupcakes leading to a grander surprise? It never hurts to hedge your bets and go big (or as big as you can reasonably afford) when it comes to romance. That said, any worthy partner will recognize and appreciate your efforts even when they don't turn out the way either party planned.

KEEPING THE ROMANCE ALIVE

Take it from Moira, a contented member of a successful decades-long marriage: the secret to a truly great relationship is to keep surprising one another. Endeavor to do something extraordinary on this most meaningful of days. Consider the kind of surprise that would delight your partner on your anniversary. Are they the kind of person to appreciate a sweet treat . . . and nothing else? Do they yearn for a little taste of shared luxury? Or do they just want the pleasure of your company? Make that wish come true for them.

Do Something Special

You can't count on your children to throw you an anniversary party. Truth be told, you can't even count on them to say "Happy Anniversary" without considerable prodding. So the planning of any special celebrations will fall to you. Luckily, lowered standards can be a real lifesaver in the surprise department. When you've been relegated to eating three meals a day at the same café—however exhaustive its menu may be—dinner at a new restaurant may be all you need to elevate the day.

Plan in Advance

A little drama can certainly help keep the spark alight, but a lot of drama can ruin an otherwise lovely experience. Avoid creating your own by arranging the day well in advance. You can't just cross your fingers and hope for a cancellation, even if you could always swing a table back in your more prosperous days. (A kind smile doesn't have quite the same effect on hostesses as cold, hard cash.) With a firm plan in place, you can also avoid undesirable invitations and awkward run-ins. Usually.

Be Mindful of Your Budget

You may not be able to pull off the elaborate anniversary celebration of years past, but you can still celebrate. Take advantage of local discounts and offers from friends. Are you really in a position to turn down a four-for-three coupon to a nice restaurant? Yes, it's less than ideal. But a delicious meal with friends can be just as lovely as dinner alone—even if those friends are Roland and Jocelyn. For one thing, that nice restaurant probably doesn't even serve fondue. And surely your friends will use utensils in public. Just don't let them choose the wine.

› CELEBRATING LONG DISTANCE

As Ted would tell you, marking a special occasion can be especially difficult when you're thousands of miles away from your partner and besieged by fire ants. But with a little planning and the help of a good friend, you can create an anniversary celebration to rival those of the most inseparable couples. Plan the evening around activities that you can enjoy together via video call, from having a romantic meal to cozying up with a sweet movie. The important thing is not letting the occasion pass you by.

Stand Up for Yourself

Standing up for yourself and your friends can be extremely sexy, so don't avoid doing so just to keep the peace on your anniversary. If you want an evening alone with your partner, say so. If you're biting your tongue about bad behavior, stop. You are responsible for making this day the most enjoyable it can be.

Enlist the Help of a Friend

Having a friend on the ground where your partner lives can make planning a surprise a piece of chocolate ganache torte. If that friend happens to be the manager of the town's only café, all the better. With a little notice, they might be able to help you transform a booth there into your own private dining experience, complete with candlelight and all of your partner's favorite nibbles. Just make sure they don't unintentionally third-wheel your date and become even more of a bucket of cold water than the fire ants.

Go All Out

This isn't your everyday video chat, with family members buzzing around and minding your business. If you're going to put together an anniversary celebration from thousands of miles away, you may as well make it count. A little extra romance to help bridge the distance never hurt anyone. You could recreate a favorite date or surprise your partner with a private car. (Consider asking a friend to be the driver, though. An unexpected chauffeur at the door could raise some red flags—especially for those, like Alexis, who've spent time in the trunk of a car in Thailand.)

❯ CELEBRATE WITH FRIENDS

Your first instinct might be to shy away from company on your anniversary. And that instinct would be correct. Trust that instinct. As Sartre famously said, "Hell is other people." But if you have to spend the evening with friends, Johnny would warn you to make sure they're the real ones and not the ones who, perhaps, left you for dead when you hit rock bottom. You might be surprised by how happy you are to celebrate with good friends by your side.

Not-Too-Salty Olive Tapenade

Tapenade goes with everything: anniversary dinners, Brie, robberies . . . you name it. Using Castelvetrano olives gives this particular tapenade a rich, buttery, and not-at-all salty flavor. Okay, yeah, it's olive tapenade. So it's going to be a little salty. But not too salty.

≫ MAKES 1½ CUPS

1 cup Castelvetrano olives, pitted

½ cup Niçoise or Kalamata olives, pitted

¼ cup lightly packed fresh flat-leaf parsley

1 tablespoon drained capers

¼ cup extra virgin olive oil

2 medium cloves garlic

1 tablespoon lemon juice

1. Combine all of the ingredients in the bowl of a food processor and pulse about 10 times before using a spatula to scrape down the sides of the bowl. (No one wants uneven chunks in their tapenade.)

2. Pulse 5 to 10 more times until everything is finely chopped and well combined.

3. Serve the tapenade in a decorative bowl, probably with some Brie. And crostini. And salami. And maybe some branzino.

chapter

14

Bachelor (ette) PARTIES

So, you've been chosen to host your dear friend's prenuptial festivities. Buckle up, because it's going to be a very bumpy ride. From fielding seven-page emails and dealing with daily feedback on your choices to helping the bachelor(ette) with, well, literally everything else going on in their life, you'll be one busy little event planner. Hopefully, you'll have someone you can lean on for the parts of party planning and general pre-wedding merriment that don't come naturally to you. Maybe that's all of it. Maybe you're a little more Stevie than you are Alexis when it comes to elegant affairs. That's okay. Just remember what an honor it is to be chosen! And keep repeating it to yourself until you make it through the ceremony.

❯ BE THERE FOR YOUR BACHELOR(ETTE)

Your number one job as the best friend of the bride or groom is to be there for them . . . even if you'd rather not be. Usually, that means offering your friend emotional support and the occasional opinion. Sometimes, it means ferrying your friend's fiancé to his wisdom-tooth removal, like Stevie does for Patrick. The bottom line is, you knew what you were getting into when you agreed to this. And maybe one day you'll get married and have a chance to ~~torture~~ honor your friend the same way.

❯ PLANNING THE EVENING

Your number two job when planning the bachelor(ette) party is to manage expectations. The soon-to-be-married often have long-held dreams about what their wedding festivities will look like. They need their friends to help them make those dreams come true. And when that's not possible—like, not even remotely—they need their friends to bring them crashing back to Earth. They might not get the bachelor(ette) party of their dreams, but they can still have a perfectly serviceable evening.

Ask for Forgiveness

Instead of permission, that is. Half the fun of hosting a bachelor(ette) party is surprising the honoree. Skip the approval process and include a few personal touches, like enlarged baby photos. Any normal person will be thrilled by the effort and thought you put into planning their party. If they're not, then you get some free entertainment for the party.

Ask the Bachelor(ette) for Input

Not everyone will be so bold as to ask the bride- or groom-to-be what they imagine for their pre-wedding revelry. But you are not everyone. You are a person who has no qualms about bringing a little reality check to that party. So let them dream! Have them outline their ideal night—*ideally* in fewer than seven pages—and then sit down with a bottle of wine and enjoy a good chuckle while you read through their insanely improbable requests.

Ignore the Bachelor(ette)'s Input

Once you have a clear picture of your friend's hopes and dreams, you can look around and lower your expectations. You will not be able to provide most of that. Or any of that. Now's the time to tell your bachelor(ette) to lower *their* expectations and do the best you can with what you've got. If that's a tradition that means the world to your friend's fiancé and a cocktail hour with their loving family, then that's not half bad.

Don't Ask for Their Input in the First Place

Sometimes, the safest thing to do is to completely avoid asking what the bachelor(ette) wants. Make the plans and tell your friend about them when it's too close to the party for them to do anything about it. How do you get away with this, you ask? Stall and obfuscate. "I've got a great surprise planned." "I'm on top of it." "You're going to love it." If they put you in charge of the party, they must have at least some trust in you. Use that misguided trust to your advantage.

❯❯ SHARING HOSTING RESPONSIBILITIES

When two people mean a lot to the bachelor(ette), it can be hard for the bride- or groom-to-be to choose which one will have the honor of standing by his/her side throughout the wedding process. That decision becomes a little less muddled when one of those people has plans to leave the country for months on end. (What are you supposed to do? Just stop planning the wedding until your sister gets back from her tropical vacation?) Their delayed departure might be a godsend for dealing with a high-maintenance bachelor(ette), though—especially if weddings aren't really your thing.

Avoid Interpersonal Conflict

A bachelor(ette)'s asking two people to host pre-wedding events together can be a minefield of egos and opposing taste. If you're feeling hurt by the perceived snub of not being your friend's (brother's) one and only, take a beat. Once you accept that you are not the only person on the team, you may find that your cohost really needed the win of being selected for such a significant honor. Alexis would tell you to be sensitive to what the other person is going through and to look for ways you can help. It's called *growth*.

Play to Your Strengths

Once you get over the initial shock of being paired up, you can start to find ways to complement each other's skill sets. Maybe one of you is better at fashion stuff while the other is better at not giving a fuck. Both skills are absolutely integral to the high-stakes game of wedding planning. Perhaps one of you has known the bachelor(ette) longer and can help make decisions while the other lives in the real world and can help manage expectations, like Stevie does for David. Divide and conquer!

❯ CHOOSING THE ACTIVITIES

Of course you want to try to give the bachelor(ette) what they want. But it's not always practical. Compromises must be made. Yes, it's a shame that you don't have the budget for a Tahitian dolphin tour. But spending the night with family and friends is what really matters. Try to extract from your friend's requests a common denominator. Are they looking for elegance? Think: signature menu. Adventure? A team-style games night might be in order. Just try to aim higher than fried cheese at the local watering hole. Even by Stevie's standards, that's bleak.

How to Beat an Escape Room

Beating an escape room takes patience, skill, intellect, and, most of all, a willingness to play the fucking game in the first place. But even the most apathetic among you may get caught up in the excitement of finding clues and solving puzzles. Who knows what epiphanies await behind that locked door?

You'll Need
Your wits
To give up your cellphones

GAME SETUP

An escape room is an immersive experience where you choose an adventure and work with a group of friends (and family) to overcome challenges and solve puzzles in an attempt to escape a locked room in less than 60 minutes.

GAME PLAY

1. Once you have the first clue, pair off into teams and take a sweep around the room. When you do find something, make everyone aware of it, preferably without violently screaming at them.

2. Keep enthusiasm high by cheering each other on after each solved puzzle. You'll need to be mindful of the time, but remember that it's just a game. No need to give yourself (or others) an anxiety attack.

3. When something isn't working, pull together to find a creative solution. And don't be afraid to ask for hints when you need them. (But, you know, after you've actually put some effort in.)

4. Remember that the sooner you solve all the puzzles and escape the room, the sooner you can get to the drinks.

chapter

15

Elegant
WEDDINGS

When you've been stuck in a small town where a hot-pink leopard-print shirt passes for elegance, it can be very tempting to pin all of your hopes and dreams on your wedding—one day that allows for, and even encourages, delusions of grandeur. Striking floral arrangements, stunning table settings, exquisite catering, and beautifully dressed guests are *de rigueur* for these events. But that kind of pageantry takes months to plan, and all it takes is one bad storm to bring that magnificent house of cards crashing to the ground. By putting your love front and center in all of your planning decisions, you can hopefully avoid a mental breakdown on your way to the altar.

CHOOSING A VENUE

Possibly the most important decision you'll make in the planning process is where you'll hold the event. Once you pick the venue, every other decision falls into place around it. The peony-and-stone-lined manor with a farm just up the road means bacon-filled canapés and black tie. A tent in a lush, green field? Wildflowers, glowing lanterns, and a pizza oven, obviously. Town hall? Well, if things are that hopeless, then it doesn't really matter what the decor looks like, does it? Just slap some twinkle lights up and call it a fucking day.

Get Pricing Up Front

Before you fall in love with a place, make sure it's within your budget—or even circling the parking lot that your 1977 Lincoln Continental of a budget is stalled in. There's nothing worse than falling completely in love with a venue only to find out that you couldn't afford it even if you and your partner each sold a kidney. And because you've already smelled the peonies and tasted the farm-fresh bacon and envisioned the wedding of your dreams taking place there, you may just be desperate enough to do it.

Be Wary of Discounts

Okay, there might be just one thing worse than falling in love with a venue you can't afford: getting a discount on that venue and then having to hear the tortured screams of farm animals while reciting your vows. When something in the wedding-planning process is heavily discounted, be suspicious. Like, David-when-Alexis-offers-to-delay-her-flight-to-the-Galápagos-so-he-can-book-the-venue suspicious. No one does anything generous just out of the goodness of their heart—not even Twyla. (Who could have paid for David and Patrick's entire wedding without breaking a sweat, by the way.)

Look for Untapped Potential

When you realize that booking a fancy venue might not be worth sacrificing other things (like your appetite for pork), you can start to see the potential in unconventional choices. With a tent and some lights, a backyard wedding can be just as beautiful as one at an elegant estate. And it's made all the more special by the memories you've shared there. Just learn from David's rain-soaked mistake: a tent is nonnegotiable when it comes to backyard events.

AVOID CONFLICTING SCHEDULES

You can't always predict the timing of major life events. But when one is already on the books, it can be helpful to keep it top of mind so that you don't, say, schedule your wedding for a day when a dear family member will be busy avoiding lizards in the Galápagos Islands. Similarly, once your date is set, make sure to remind forgetful family members of it often. Had David given Moira a save-the-date to display, she might have thought to push her start date and been able to snag the lie-flat seats after all.

SETTING THE MENU

You want people talking about three things at your wedding: 1) how amazing you looked, 2) how happy you are together, and 3) how incredible the food was. Those first two are a given, but the third is no small feat. No one goes to a wedding so they can do the chicken dance and make small talk with their tablemates. They want to be wined and dined. And you want to avoid hearing about the dry chicken on your anniversary every year. Spend some time and a little extra money making good menu choices.

Set the Right Tone

Do you want your wedding to say "elegant Gatsby-esque affair" or "backyard barbecue by Roland"? Because the sight of macaroni-and-cheese in a chafing dish can instantly pollute the air of tasteful sophistication you've been striving for. Choose a caterer who understands your vision for the event and has plenty of complementary options available, then set aside time to sample those options. No one's going to be talking about the lobster roll if it isn't as beautifully plated as it is delicious.

Understand Your Budget

When you're responsible for the cost of the catering, you can easily look at your budget and realize that the pizza oven is completely out of the question. Be just as mindful about the budget when someone else has been kind enough to offer to pay. You certainly can't assume that they have unlimited funds to put toward crème brûlée, no matter how incredibly delicious and essential to the evening's aesthetic it may be. Open communication is key to finding a culinary compromise everyone can be happy with.

》 SAVOR THE PLANNING STAGE

If you save all of your enjoyment for the wedding day, you could miss out on some wonderful memories. David and Patrick will forever remember the time Patrick accidentally spray-tanned himself to look like a cheese puff, or the time he accidentally ordered David an erotic massage. You can't plan for things like that. You just have to soak them in when they happen. (Plus, the planning stage may be your only opportunity for years to walk through manicured gardens and eat truffle-topped salads. So take advantage of that.)

》 REMEMBER WHAT'S IMPORTANT

At the end of the wedding day, it's really not the venue or the catering that's important. It's getting to end that day married to your own personal Mariah Carey. And remembering that will help you hold it together when things inevitably go to shit. Although you may not be forced to abandon most of your hard work and re-plan the wedding in a matter of hours, no wedding goes off without a hitch. So take a deep breath and remember to enjoy your happy ending.

How to Handle Things When It All Goes to Shit

There comes a point in every wedding when you have to throw out the mood board and just do what you can with what you have. When that happens, focus on the things you can control and the happy ending that's waiting for you. (The cocktail. At the end of this chapter.)

You'll Need
Friends and family who love you
(or at least your fiancé)
A massage

MAKING IT WORK

1. First and foremost, stay calm. Have a cup of tea, eat a few bagels, get a massage. You don't want to see a worried face in your wedding pictures.

2. Ask for help from friends and family. Surely someone you know has been ordained by the Universal Church of Google.

3. Find any dry, available space to hold the ceremony. Perhaps someone knows the florist and can secure extra flowers and curtains to obscure the sadness of your new venue.

4. Enjoy your day. Even if it's a complete shit show, it's still your shit show.

Prioritize Practicality

This is your wedding—
an event that happens
once in a lifetime
(twice if you're Pat Sajak).
You get to be a little
aspirational in your planning.
But don't lose sight of the garden for the peonies. This is about marrying the love of your life. And if you'd like to do that rain or shine, you're going to need a tent more than you need a pizza oven and an officiant with a reliable mode of transportation more than a haikuist who rides a penny-farthing. Make good choices.

Accept Honeymoon Hospitality

Take it from Stevie and Jake: If someone wants to give you free Champagne and cover your bed in rose petals, don't look a gift horse in the mouth. Put on that "Newlywed" sash and smile for your fellow diners. Sure, you'd feel better about it if you actually were newlyweds. But it's really the staff's fault for not verifying these things.

Include the Right People

On your big day, who would you rather have by your side: the people who've been there all along, or the ones who disappeared when things got hard? Looking back, you may not remember whether your fair-weather friends from New York showed up. But you will definitely remember if you got married without your sister . . . because she will never let you forget it. So make room for the people who mean the most to you and tell that table of New Yorkers to go fuck themselves—they don't deserve your beef tenderloin.

The Happy Ending

Whether it's held at the town hall or a graceful manor house, no wedding would be complete without a signature cocktail. This homage to Patrick and David delightfully combines bright citrus with hints of rose and bitterness. (And no one will know how cheap the gin is when it's mixed with all this other stuff.)

≫ SERVES 1

FOR THE COCKTAIL
1 cardamom pod
2 ounces gin
1 ounce ruby red grapefruit juice
1 ounce lemon juice
½ ounce rose simple syrup
2 dashes Peychaud's bitters
Ice cubes
Rose petal, for garnish

FOR THE ROSE SIMPLE SYRUP
1 cup water
½ cup food-grade rose water
1 cup sugar
1 heaping cup rose petals, rinsed

1. To make the rose simple syrup, combine the water, rose water, sugar, and rose petals in a small saucepan over medium heat. Stir and heat until the sugar has dissolved, then remove the mixture from the heat and let it cool to room temperature. Reserve ½ ounce for this recipe and store the rest in an airtight container in your mini fridge for up to 1 month.

2. Should your motel room have a working toaster oven, lightly toast the cardamom pod.

3. In a mortar and pestle or clean Solo cup, gently muddle (crush) the pod using just enough pressure to crack it and a few of its seeds.

4. Add the crushed pod and the rest of the ingredients to a cocktail shaker, top with ice, and shake well, being careful not to take your many frustrations out on the gin.

5. Strain the cocktail over ice into any clean glass and garnish with a rose petal.

chapter

16

Holiday PARTIES

You may be used to holiday parties that make Page Six, but that doesn't mean you can't enjoy an intimate little get-together. Last minute. Amid Christmas-tree surge pricing, and with very few resources and almost no cooperation from the family you're desperately trying to create new memories with. It's the holidays—miracles happen. It doesn't matter whether you light a menorah, decorate a tree, or mix traditions. The holidays are about family and friends coming together, enjoying each other's company, and being grateful for what life has given them. By pulling together to pull this off, you'll have started an even better tradition than any that came before it.

EMBRACING TRADITION

When you look back at the holidays you've celebrated over your life, it's often the traditions that stand out in your mind and make you feel connected to the season and to each other. But you should focus on embracing the ones that mean the most to you. Johnny would tell you that Paul Shaffer accompanying your wife and son on the piano is one hell of a memory. But it's not as good as listening to your wife softly sing carols in the warm glow of friendship and community. That's something you'll look forward to year after year.

See Your Past Clearly

Especially where holidays are concerned, it can be tempting to look back at the past with rosé-colored glasses. Nostalgia, wine, and Christmas pills mix to create a fuzzy, happy memory—at least for Moira. But if you take the time to think about those holidays gone by, you may start to realize they weren't quite as happy as you thought. Each year, you have a chance to start fresh, create different traditions, and make new memories. But only if you're honest about needing to improve on the past.

Start New Traditions

Traditions are about looking forward, not back. What will you want your holiday celebrations to look like next year, and the year after that? What new traditions can you start today that you'll treasure tomorrow? Maybe it's buying the saddest looking Christmas tree on the lot and fixing it up as a family. Perhaps it's heading to the café for a milkshake with your partner (a boozy one, though, obviously). Start a tradition of doing whatever makes you and your family truly grateful to be celebrating the holiday.

PLAN EARLY

Because both decorations and friends become scarcer the closer you get to the holiday, it's best to begin planning your holiday party several weeks in advance. People have lives, obligations, their boyfriend's judgy friends to impress. You can't expect them to drop everything just because you're suddenly filled with the holiday spirit. Although some, like Roland, require just a week's notice, most will need more. Whatever you do, don't start planning the day of the event and expect a miracle. That only happens in TV shows.

LAST-MINUTE PLANNING

When you do inevitably decide to leave everything until the last minute, you're going to need to keep your spirits high. You have an impossible task ahead of you. With the help of family, friends, and wine, you can make it happen. Letting everyone know why this party is so important to you can go a long way toward motivating them to help you pull it off. If it seems like a whim (because, you know, the party is in six hours from now), they may not take it very seriously.

Pull Together

Breaking the party planning down into tasks and dividing those tasks among family members can help things move more quickly. But it's essential that everyone understand and welcome their assignment so you don't have to use someone's drunken strumpet of a grandmother's old Mardi Gras beads as tree trimmings and celebrate the holiday in a room devoid of guests. Put the person with the best taste in charge of decorations, and make sure your PR person is awake when you ask them to handle the guest list.

Make Sure It's Memorable

A successful soirée is one you both remember and delight in remembering. Avoid taking your Christmas pills until you've taken a moment to savor the evening—the lights, the decorations, the friends you're sharing it with. You might look back on that moment with fondness for years to come, realizing only then how lucky you were.

Make Sure There's Wine

No holiday would be complete without spirits! And wine. Go ahead—open the wine early. It's fine. (Take a sip.) Everything's fine. (And another.) It's all going *very* smoothly. (Just one more.) If you're feeling optimistic, grab at least a case of wine for guests. And if you're a fan of Stevie's holiday tradition, grab another case just for you. Just make sure you offer something else to line your guests' stomachs. Festively decorated homemade cookies are always a hit, even if they were baked with well-intentioned lies as well as love.

Make the Space Festive

Having a connection in the home decor world can be a huge help in getting the party together quickly. If they choose to help, that is. You really can't begrudge a person an espresso machine when they're saving up for it like a responsible adult (possibly for the first time in their life). But the espresso machine can wait. The party cannot. Because it's in three hours. So now's not the time to be a cheap ass—get those decorations up. Just try not to create fire hazards in the process.

〉 CHERISH EACH OTHER

At the end of the day, holidays are not about fancy decorations, ice sculptures, grand pianos, or celebrity guests. They're about celebrating with the people you love. Whether you pull off a last-minute party or simply spend a few minutes savoring the holiday with your family, you know now what's important to you. And you can celebrate that every day of the year.

Christmas Eve Meatloaf

When things don't go the way you'd hoped, you, like Mr. Rose, might reach for the comfort of your regular Tuesday-night meal. Even if it's Wednesday and that meal has to be reheated. Hey, that's the beauty of a food like meatloaf—it's just as comforting the second time around.

» SERVES 10

FOR THE MEATLOAF
1 pound 90% lean ground beef
1 cup dried breadcrumbs
½ cup diced yellow onion
½ cup milk
1 large egg, beaten
2 tablespoons ketchup
1 tablespoon Worcestershire sauce
1 teaspoon dried parsley leaves
¾ teaspoon kosher salt
½ teaspoon garlic powder
¼ teaspoon freshly ground black pepper

FOR THE GLAZE
¼ cup ketchup
2 tablespoons packed light brown sugar
1 tablespoon red wine vinegar

1. Preheat the oven to 350°F.

2. To make the meatloaf, add all the meatloaf ingredients to a large bowl and use your hands to mix them together until well combined.

3. Transfer the meat mixture to a large loaf pan (9 x 5 x 3 inches) and push it down to fill the pan and create a flat top.

4. To make the glaze, add the glaze ingredients to a small bowl and stir to combine. Then spread the glaze evenly over the top of the meatloaf.

5. Transfer the pan to the oven and bake the meatloaf, uncovered, for 55 minutes. Then remove it from the oven and let it rest for 8 to 10 minutes before slicing and serving.

chapter

17

Business
SOIRÉES

Impressing colleagues and potential investors isn't easy, but it
is still just a form of entertaining. From hosting an exploratory
dinner to speaking at a small conference or presenting at a
large firm, you are doing little more than ensuring that your
guests are enjoying themselves. Except in these cases, you're
also ensuring that you get what you need from the event.
This sort of entertaining shouldn't be left to just anyone.
As Moira and Johnny prove time and again, closing a deal
requires a deftness that doesn't come naturally to most. And
sometimes—especially when cheese is involved—it doesn't
come naturally to them, either. No matter what happens,
hold onto your optimism. You'll need it.

⟫ TRAVEL ARRANGEMENTS

Taking control of your destiny begins with your travel arrangements. No one should be forced to suffer four hours in a truck with Roland singing along to Lynyrd Skynyrd—Moira is absolutely right to try to make alternate arrangements. But one should always accept an invitation to use a private plane. Accepting luxury shows your potential investor that you are worthy of luxury. Also, they have free booze. That's a big step above carpooling, where you have to (and should) bring your own flask.

⟫ THE RIGHT HEADSPACE

Preparing for a meeting requires more than just working on your short game. You need to understand the people you'll be speaking to, the kind of information they're interested in, and the outcome you're hoping for. But most of all, you need confidence—in your pitch and in yourself. Preferably both. If you can only have one, though, have confidence in yourself. You'll never convince a room full of people to believe in you if you don't believe in yourself. March straight past that name-tag table and into the hearts and minds of your audience.

Skip the Name Tag

No matter what Roland says, suiting up for an important business meeting should never include wearing accessories with adhesive backing. The only acceptable name tag is an enamel pin worn as a welcoming touch for paying customers. If your presentation is any good, a name tag will be redundant. And if it's not, you'll prefer the anonymity.

Know Who You're Talking To

The first step in this little dance is to understand what matters most to your audience. Do you need to tend to fragile egos in a room full of small-town somebodies? Or indulge the fragile egos of investors who were too stupid to fund the biggest ridesharing company in the world? Perhaps you need to slap the fragile ego out of a former costar and demand what you're worth. (There are a lot of fragile egos in business.) Knowing who you're speaking to allows you to talk up the value of your proposal in a language they'll understand.

See the Big Picture

Once you know who you're speaking to, you need to speak to their issues. Take a lesson in acting from Moira: Whether you're securing funding for town activities or investors for an ambitious business venture, get in touch with your motivation for doing so. Consider the importance of what you're doing. Then, when you're speaking to your audience, channel someone who cares about those things. The more it feels like you care, the more they will care.

❯ UNDERSTANDING THE SITUATION

If you're going to properly prepare for a meeting, you need to know exactly what you're walking into. Leave nothing about your meeting to chance if you can help it. Travel arrangements, timing, activities, presentation equipment, attendees—take nothing for granted. The last thing you want is to show up with a golf stick (as Stevie affectionately calls it) in hand only for it to end up leaning against a chair, unused, in a sad, brown dining room. But then, when you've got nothing left to lose, you've got everything to gain.

Clarify the Details

Whether you're hosting the meeting or simply attending it, it's important to talk through all the details and manage expectations—yours and theirs. Would Johnny show up at the golf course in his windbreaker if he knew the meeting would be held indoors? Of course not. And his usual tailored suit might have left a better impression on the club managers. Get all the details, then confirm them again shortly before arriving. That gives the other attendees the opportunity to communicate any changes in plans, like sudden weeklong trips to South Africa.

Read the Room

Being able to read the room is an art, and one that comes in very handy during business meetings. Pay attention to how people are receiving your message, watching for subtle clues like stifled laughter and rolled eyes. But don't lose hope if the audience seems uninterested. Look around for the one eager face in the bunch of slack-jawed frat boys. By speaking directly to the right person, you may land yourself an even better opportunity.

Ask for What You Want

As Mr. Rose wisely wrote, "You miss 100 percent of the tapes you don't play." If you don't take a shot, you have absolutely no chance of getting what you want. Ask for that round of golf, that multimillion-dollar investment, that diamond tennis bracelet. What's the worst that can happen? More importantly, what's the best? Your entire life could change in a moment because you took a chance, went after what you wanted, and gave it your all.

DRINK IN MODERATION

Don't be too quick to pop that Champagne. Remember that endorphins are an upper and can be absolutely devastating when combined with alcohol. Just imagine if, like Moira, you were to end up in the wrong bed and not only miss out on your one chance to enjoy the amenities of a real hotel but also pass out next to a naked Roland Schitt. Devastating. In all aspects of business, from daily operation to special events, it's really best to keep the drinking to a minimum.

Sparkling White Russian

There's nothing quite like a cocktail with new friends to celebrate a successful business meeting, and surely one drink can't hurt. Unlike the version they serve at the Diamond Club, Moira would consider this Sparkling White Russian quite potable. Just sip it slowly and tell Gavin to fuck off when he comes around with the hard stuff.

≫ SERVES 1

1 ounce vodka
1 ounce coffee liqueur
1 ounce half-and-half
Float of cola to top

1. Fill a rocks glass with ice.

2. Stir in the vodka and coffee liqueur, then pour in the half-and-half and float the cola on the top.

chapter

18

Town-Wide
EVENTS

-College-

PUBIC RELATIONS

Like Alexis's Singles' Week, a town-wide event is one that utilizes and benefits the entire town. Maybe it brings together the residents, or maybe it brings in new visitors. It definitely gets everyone involved in planning and enjoying the event. A town-wide event is not an easy thing to pull off, but it is one of the most rewarding kinds of events to plan. Alexis would tell you that the most important thing when organizing something this big is to have faith in your own abilities. You may not have had to escape from a Thai drug lord's trunk, but surely there have been plenty of times in your life when you've had to perform under pressure and you've done it. You can do this, too. And the town will be so much better off for it.

START WITH THE RIGHT IDEA

Planning starts with having the right idea—one that will interest people and benefit the town. And one you can actually manage. Start small, maybe playing off a concept that's been successful in other towns. But start before you feel ready, too. Because whether you know it or not, you *are* ready. Don't let anyone tell you otherwise or discourage you from sharing your concept. There will be plenty of people who see your idea for the stroke of brilliance it is. (Plus, the naysayers might just have their own agenda.)

APPLY FOR PERMITS AND GRANTS

It's not like you're putting on a town-wide event out of the goodness of your own heart and wallet. You need money. And that means going through the proper channels with your plan in hand and getting the town's approval. If you can prove that your event can generate interest and profits, you should have no problem getting the council on board. Just don't leave it to chance or other people—apply for approval in person and make your case. That way no one can *misinterpret* your proposal.

NAILING DOWN THE DETAILS

Learn from Moira's many experiences with elaborate fundraisers: any worthwhile event will require a meticulously kept plan book. From guest accommodations to activities and promotions, there's a lot of details to account for when it comes to an event like this—especially when that event is encouraging an influx of visitors. As the event planner, you'll need to work out all of those details. Check in with any cohosts often, but make sure you're the one holding the book.

Test the Products

People are coming from far and wide to participate in your event, and the last thing you want is for one of your activities to make the front page of neighboring newspapers for the wrong reasons. Check out every experience you plan to offer to your attendees and make sure that they all work well within the theme of the event. (The venue falling through for the sloppy-Joe-eating contest was probably a blessing in disguise for Alexis's Singles Week.) Immerse yourself in the experience. Just don't let your competitive spirit—or jealousy—take the wheel. This isn't about you.

Offer Local Incentives

Getting local businesses involved in the event benefits everyone—the business, the town, and the participants. Consider what offerings and promotions make the most sense for your event, then run your ideas past the vendors and get their feedback. No one knows their business like they do. If not for Twyla, Alexis might have accidentally encouraged singles to eat alone for the half-off discount rather than helping them pair up with a two-for-one promo (proving, actually, that two heads are better than one).

Plan Carefully

You never know what could go wrong at the last minute, so make sure you have all your adoptable, sweater-clad puppies in a row early on. Meet with volunteers regularly, even constantly, to keep things organized. And never leave things for the day of the event. If you do, you could find yourself needing to improvise and giving a heartfelt speech about your relationship to a group of total strangers. If, like Alexis, you thrive under pressure, you might come up with something even better, though.

⟩ ON THE DAY

The day of the event can be as nerve-racking as it is exciting for host and attendees alike. But it's even more nerve-racking if you aren't ready to roll with the punches. It's your job to make sure that the event starts on time and unfolds smoothly, no matter what's going on around you. Maybe you have to help a friend evict a family of angry raccoons from their living room, or you have to come up with a new activity on the fly. That's just the high-stakes world of event planning.

Expect the Unexpected

Nothing will ever go smoothly 100 percent of the time. Make sure you have contingency plans for any unexpected bumps in the event-planning road. When a venue falls through, for instance, ask yourself whose spacious home you can borrow. Hopefully you can find a space that you didn't unintentionally destroy with your own negligence, but maybe you just roll up your sleeves and help clear out those dead plants. Or offer moral support while your friend rolls up their sleeves, as Alexis does for Mutt. Whatever happens, you make it work.

Enjoy Yourself

Savoring the planning process is easier said than done, especially if this is your first event. But take a moment now and again to appreciate how far you've come. A few weeks earlier, this event was just a thought in your head. With the help of friends and family and the support of the town, it's blossomed into a beautiful reality. Appreciate that. And remember, just because you're hosting the event doesn't mean you can't participate in it. Hand that clipboard off to your eager cohost, and enjoy!

Sloppy Jocelyns

Love is messy, but there's no need to make it worse by shoveling sloppy joes into your mouth in front of potential partners. Shame-eat these incredible sandwiches in private, like a normal person.

⟩ SERVES 6

1 tablespoon unsalted butter

1 teaspoon olive oil

1 pound 90% lean ground beef

⅓ large green bell pepper, minced

½ large yellow onion, minced

3 medium cloves garlic, minced

1 tablespoon tomato paste

⅔ cup ketchup

⅓ cup water

1 tablespoon brown sugar

1 teaspoon yellow mustard

¾ teaspoon chili powder

½ teaspoon Worcestershire sauce

½ teaspoon kosher salt

¼ teaspoon red pepper flakes

¼ teaspoon freshly ground black pepper

6 buns

1. Add the butter and oil to a large pan over medium heat and let the butter melt. Add the beef to the pan, stirring to break it apart, and cook until browned, about 5 minutes. Transfer it to a paper towel–lined plate to drain.

2. Add the bell pepper and onion to the same pan and cook until soft, 2 to 3 minutes. Then stir in the garlic and let it cook until fragrant, about 30 seconds.

3. Transfer the browned beef back to the pan and stir in the tomato paste. Then stir in the ketchup, water, brown sugar, mustard, chili powder, Worcestershire sauce, salt, red pepper flakes, and black pepper until everything is well combined.

4. Let the beef mixture continue to cook and thicken for 10 to 15 minutes before dividing it among the buns, or shovel it directly into your mouth from the pan while hunched over the stove.

chapter

19

Campaign EVENTS

Even in the smallest of towns, running for office can be a daunting endeavor. Running against a beloved resident of the town and wife of the current mayor? That's an even more unenviable task if there ever was one. It takes an indomitable spirit to succeed under those terms, and Moira Rose is just the person to show you how to do it. From declaring her intention to run and making herself more approachable to reaching out to potential constituents, her campaign was a master class in acting your way into office. Just imagine the things you can accomplish from within—planter boxes as far as the eye can see! Just remember not to underestimate your opponent, no matter how feeble-minded they may seem.

 GET IN THE RACE

Before you officially enter your bid for office, make sure that this race is one you actually want to win. Understand the obligations (and the length of the term) to which you're committing. You certainly wouldn't want to come to regret your decision immediately upon your victory, like Moira does. Of course, she does many great things while in office that make the win worthwhile, including helping Rose Apothecary and Singles' Week get off the ground. With a bit of pluck and determination, you too can wire the town for your family's success.

GREETING THE PUBLIC

Your first public appearance after your official announcement should be a memorable one—but preferably because of your platform. A candidate's breakfast is the perfect setting for introducing yourself to your potential constituents and answering any questions they may have about your positions. But remember that, from what you wear to what you say, every interaction you have will be parsed by the local papers and your opponents to try to skew public opinion. Strive to make an impression that won't soon leave the voters' minds.

Dress to Impress

Dressing to impress in a small town is very different than doing so in well-traveled circles. An unusual outfit can make you the talk of the town, but it may not win you votes. That's why the things you wear to these early public appearances should be more accessible than aspirational. You don't have to shop at Blouse Barn. You do, however, need people to get to know you if they're to vote for you. And they can't get to know you if they feel they need to shout over your gold lamé jumpsuit.

Be Approachable

Once you've nailed the fashion, you need to focus on the culture. Try to act like the common folk do, from sharing in their gossip to delighting in their cheese-filled diets. Like a predator closing in on its prey, try to blend into your surroundings to entice your unsuspecting meal to tread closer. But also remember that you need these people to like you. So when they do come close, resist the urge to pounce on their faults. Simply pointing out that you're on their side might do the trick.

Bring the Booze

Ahh, the great uniter. Nothing breaks the ice quite like vodka. Bring a bottle and plenty of cups to your next event and let the chin-wagging commence. Before long, you'll all have forgotten there ever was a cultural divide. And then you can get to the real campaigning—subtly disparaging your opponent to make *them* seem like the power-hungry outsider. This is a battle of wits, and you can't help it if your opponent is outgunned.

❯❯ INTIMATE GATHERINGS

Once you've gotten past the initial meet-and-greets, you'll need to have more in-depth conversations with your potential constituents. At these more intimate gatherings, you can get to know your voters, the issues that affect them, and how they expect you to help. And they can discern how well suited you are to the task. As a lifelong resident of the town, your opponent will surely have an advantage here. But you can bring a breath of fresh air to the stale state of local politics and its nepotistic ways. You just have to let the voters know it.

Ask for Help

Knowing your own limitations and delegating to those who are better equipped is the only path to success in politics. There's nothing wrong with asking for help. Except if you're asking your opponent's son for fashion advice, knowing that he has both a compulsive need to offer it and an overly dramatic mother who will not react well to it.

Host a "Schmoozefest"

As Roland and Jocelyn demonstrate (surprisingly skillfully) when they drop off colorful leftover cupcakes for Moira and Johnny, local politics is all about shaking hands and collecting checks. Hosting or attending a campaign event with the specific purpose of meeting a select group of open-eared voters can mean life or death for a struggling campaign. Now more than ever, you need to be relatable, engaged, and knowledgeable. So, when those voters bring up the struggle of balancing business and family, consider avoiding any mention of household staff. Turn, instead, to those things you have in common.

Know Your Audience

Never make assumptions about the voters. In fact, if you have any lingering questions, get clarification about the nature of your audience *before* you attend the event. Not only will this help you speak to their issues, but it will also help you avoid any uncomfortable blunders, like assuming you're speaking to a group of lesbians when you're speaking to a group of businesswomen. Should you make such a mistake, take another lesson from Moira: toss out the prepared speech and answer questions instead. Voters will appreciate your candor.

⟩⟩ AVOID OBVIOUS SUBTERFUGE

One thing that Johnny and Moira learn by way of their campaign is never to underestimate one's opponent—even if that opponent is Roland. You won't get anywhere in politics by playing fair, but you can't be caught playing dirty. Luckily for you, there is a middle ground where all the best politicians dawdle. Without making a single accusation, you can line up the dominoes and let the voters set them in motion. Shaming your opponent into dropping out of the race may not feel as good as winning outright, but . . . No, never mind. It does.

Incredible Spinach Dip

Ronnie's taste is a big step up from Roland's, so it would only make sense that her dairy-filled creations would bring a little something extra to the table—like vegetables. Perhaps that's why Johnny enjoys this dip so much. That, or he just needed something besides his foot to put in his mouth at her party.

≫ SERVES 8

8 ounces cream cheese, softened

¼ cup sour cream

¼ cup mayonnaise

1 medium clove garlic, minced

⅔ cup finely shredded Parmesan cheese

½ cup finely shredded mozzarella cheese

Freshly ground black pepper, to taste

1 (14-ounce) can quartered artichoke hearts

6 ounces frozen spinach, thawed

Tortilla chips, crackers, or
   crostini, for serving

1. Preheat the oven to 350°F and grease a 1-quart baking dish.

2. In a large bowl, combine the cream cheese, sour cream, mayonnaise, garlic, Parmesan, mozzarella, and pepper.

3. Drain and squeeze the artichokes and spinach to remove any excess liquid, then roughly chop the artichokes. Stir the artichokes and spinach into the cream cheese mixture.

4. Spread the dip evenly into the prepared baking dish, and bake until heated through and melted, about 20 minutes.

5. Serve the dip warm with tortilla chips, crackers, or crostini to the delight of guests who've had their fill of cheeseballs.

Movie
PREMIERES

Planning your own premiere isn't ideal, but it's certainly better to have a small-town premiere than no premiere at all. And should you be lucky enough to have a friend or daughter dipping her toes into the ice-cold waters of public relations, you'll barely have to do any planning at all. As the star of the film, you will of course need to lend both a guiding hand and an aura of celebrity to the event. That you'll need to prepare an outfit worthy of your status as the shining beacon of fashion and sophistication in a sea of denim-clad philistines—complete with accessories—is a given. But if your little fledgling is going to fly, you'll need to give her a good push from the nest and let her discover her own wings while she does the heavy lifting for the evening.

DRESS FOR THE OCCASION

One of the first things you can do to set the tone for your premiere is to put together your ensemble for the evening. It doesn't matter whether you can only afford to shop off the rack. It matters that you feel amazing in the outfit you choose. Also, that it looks good on camera. In fact, that might be more important than how you feel. Anyway, don't forget to purchase shoes and accessories that complete the ensemble. The right headdress can make all the difference, especially against a backdrop of guests dressed in Moira's suggested black-tie casual.

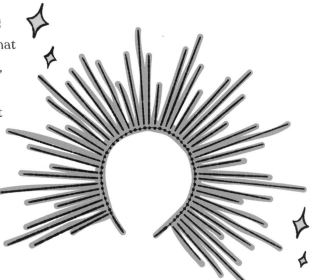

DEALING WITH TEMPERAMENTAL TALENT

With just one positive review, your quiet little viewing party can transform into a headline-grabbing premiere event. Alexis would tell you that there's no point in arguing with the star of the movie, even if she happens to be your mom. Just accept the ridiculous position you've been put in and get shit done. She'd also remind you that you've probably been in worse situations than having to put together a last-minute movie premiere attended by the same people who would drink Twyla's smoothies without asking any questions.

DESIGNING THE EVENT

As events go, movie premieres are pretty straightforward. You need a red carpet for the stars to walk (or as close as you can get to one), seating, a big screen with a working projector, and press to write about it. But if you want to make headlines with a small-town premiere, you're going to need to do things a little differently. Of course, you might not really have a choice in the matter if you're only given four hours to pull the whole thing off.

Do What You Need to Do

When you have a lot to do, little time to do it, and cameras on the way, you don't have the bandwidth for naysayers. Ask friends and town officials for help, and if they give you any pushback, remind them what's in it for them. Then lower your expectations, because there's only so much anyone can do in four hours. If a liquor license, a merlot carpet, and untrained birds are the best you can get on short notice, then at least you have the liquor license.

Get the Word Out

Throwing your own premiere is definitely a headline-worthy concept, but it'll only get the attention of the press if someone brings it to the press's attention. A local outlet is better than nothing. Think about who you know with connections in the media and ask them to extend an invitation. If you want to make headlines, though, you need a hook. Alexis's idea may have had its flaws, but you can't argue with its results.

Avoid Live Animals

Creating an immersive experience for a horror film doesn't have to mean traumatizing guests and animals alike. Will using live animals grab headlines? Sure. Will it be worth the trauma and potential lawsuits? Maybe. But there are better ways than that to create a memorable night. Instead of focusing on the crows who were doing the terrorizing, for example, Alexis might have hired some feathered actors to play their victims. The point is that you just have to get creative. And also, rethink hiring people you've met through Roland.

Encourage Good Behavior

A small-town movie premiere may be more exciting to some than to others, resulting in some problematic behavior. Remind attendees to keep things moving on the merlot carpet and only take medication that was prescribed to them. Abiding by these guidelines can help guests escape potentially disfiguring live-animal attacks. (Seriously, though—no live animals.)

⟩⟩ AT THE EVENT

Once everything's in place, it's time to let the stars of the night have their moment. And that includes anyone you bartered with to make this night happen on short notice. Factor in extra time to allow any newbies to savor their walk on the merlot carpet. But once the star arrives, it's time to move things along. A few pictures, a quick speech, and then—if you've learned anything from Alexis's debacle—move straight to the screening. When throwing things together last minute, it's really better not to tempt fate with a lot of fanfare.

Do Things Your Way

When hosting your own premiere, you have a chance to do things a little differently than you would at a major Hollywood event. For Alexis, that means letting Roland walk the almost-crimson carpet in skinny jeans. For Moira, it means walking alongside her doting husband rather than ten feet in front of him. Pulling off the impossible—whether that's turning a garbage movie into a hit or putting on a glamorous event in a few hours—gives you the right to make your own rules.

Embrace Happy Accidents

Angry crows dive-bombing your red-carpet event may not have been on your flip chart, but it is certainly a headline-grabbing event. And all press is good press, especially if you can get two wine-soaked morning-show hosts to smile through words like "severed earlobe" in front of the entire country. If your actual nightmare of a premiere has captured the nation's attention, put on a smile, take a bow, and pretend it was completely intentional. You might be surprised at how far that happy accident will get you.

Old Hollywood Cocktail

Once you have the liquor license in hand, you'll need a signature cocktail for the evening. Sure, you could go with something bloody and dystopian. But isn't it better to bring a touch of Hollywood glamour to a small town in desperate need of it? (Ronnie clearly thinks so.)

⟫ SERVES 1

FOR THE COCKTAIL
2 ounces whiskey
1 ounce freshly squeezed grapefruit juice
½ ounce honey syrup
Ice
Grapefruit peel, for garnish

FOR THE HONEY SYRUP
½ cup honey
½ cup water

1. To make the honey syrup, combine the honey and water in a small saucepan over medium heat. Stir and heat until the honey is dissolved, then remove the mixture from the heat and let it cool to room temperature. Reserve ½ ounce for this recipe and store the rest in an airtight container in your mini fridge for up to 1 month.

2. To make the cocktail, add the whiskey, grapefruit juice, and honey syrup to a cocktail shaker full of ice and shake it vigorously for 30 seconds. Pour the mixture through a fine-mesh strainer over a coupe glass (because pulp is not glamorous), and garnish the glass with the grapefruit peel.

chapter

21

Rebranding ROLLOUTS

You can't argue with a high school textbook—a rollout is a great way to give your business the fresh start it needs to bring in more high-quality customers. And although Mr. Rose isn't familiar with the term until Alexis teaches it to him, he knows a good idea when he hears one. Cleaning things up, bringing in personal touches, and actively working on your public image can only help your business succeed. Sure, you can do these things quietly over time. But since when do the Roses do anything quietly (or patiently)? A formal rollout gives you a clean slate and a blueprint you can follow all the way to the bank. If you do it correctly, that is. Maybe start by boning up on your poisonous plants.

MAKING CHANGES

When making changes to your current business, ask yourself what will appeal most to your customers. Put yourself in their shoes. Unless, of course, you've been living in those Italian-leather Oxfords yourself for the last four years. Then just think about the things that might have made that long, torturously slow walk a little easier. Focus on small changes that can have the biggest impact for your brand, like appealing to the senses with beautiful packaging, attractive decor, fragrant flowers, and comfortable facilities. Just make sure that none of those things gives your customers lice or a disfiguring rash, and you should be fine.

Spruce Things Up

Making sure that your business is rollout-ready means doing more than just sweeping the cobwebs off the ceiling mirrors. It means making sure you have a working water heater, functional Wi-Fi, thoroughly cleaned spaces, and pretty little touches like well-packaged toiletries or manicured planters. It probably also means taking down the ceiling mirrors, because this isn't the '70s. And, as Johnny would warn you, you don't want to be attracting certain regional-accounting-conference attendees who prefer to pay by the hour while trying to elevate your business's standing in the community.

Increase the Comfort Level

Once the space is clean and the decor settled, focus on making your customers as comfortable as possible. For the motel, soft, monogrammed towels and linens that don't smell like cigarette smoke are a step in the right direction. New mattresses on the beds might be a bit aspirational for the first rollout, but there's always next time. No matter what kind of business you run, make sure that you're putting the needs of your guests first. As Moira learns, even a man's request for a cot on which to lay out his clothes is perfectly valid. Absurd. But valid.

Tempt Their Taste Buds

Never underestimate the powerful pull of both smell and taste when it comes to your business. Like offering fresh popcorn at a video-rental store, appealing to the senses is all about making customers feel at home. Just like candles in a retail store can make shoppers feel at ease, the smell of freshly baked cinnamon buns and potable coffee wafting out of a motel lobby can make all the difference to a potential guest.

BUYING BRANDED MERCHANDISE

Rebranding is a big part of any rollout and allows you to completely distance yourself from the iterations of the business that came before. Updating the business name, commissioning signature products, using your logo throughout the space, and customizing marketing materials can all go a long way toward reaching new and better customers. But you do need to be careful when ordering new products, especially if they'll be custom made for you. Typos and misplaced trust can cost you.

Test the Products

If Johnny and David learn anything from the motel rollout, it's to test every new batch of product that walks through your door to ensure it meets your standards for quality and safety. Or that fathers and sons shouldn't work together. It's one of those. But the lesson *you* should take from it is really to have at least

Don't Beat a Gift Horse

When you're running a rollout for a fledgling enterprise, it can be helpful to call in favors from local vendors—especially when those vendors are family members living in that fledgling enterprise. Just remember that favors aren't business transactions and berating the vendor (or outright accusing them of negligence) rarely bodes well for the relationship post-rollout.

a Cub Scout level of knowledge about poisonous plants. David may be able to talk his vendor down, but Johnny's unfamiliarity with poison oak cost him an excellent line of signature products.

Proofread Marketing Materials

The right marketing materials pay for themselves, but only if you make sure they have the correct information on them. Or, really, any information at all. Customers can't psychically divine your social media handles, nor do they want to try. So figure out the Tweetbook before you put anything in print. Better yet, run your copy past someone who actually knows what they're doing, like a daughter who lives on social media and is starting her own communications company. Or literally anyone under the age of forty-five.

FOLLOW US ON TWEETBOOK!

MOTEL

LEAVE US A REVIEW!

⟫ INVITE A VVIP

Inviting the right person to be your first customer can have a huge impact on your marketing success, especially if you've struggled with bad reviews from fussy cot-requesters in the past. Look for someone with a large audience who doesn't mind that you're in the early phases of your rollout. But whatever you do, resist the urge to use a plant. Any reviewer worth their salt can see right through it, mostly because no one you know is a good enough actor to pull it off.

⟫ INVEST IN YOURSELF

As Johnny learns from his menacing flower arrangements, cheaping out will always come back to bite you in the ass. Or leave you with an itchy, disgusting rash on your face. Either way, not pleasant. Johnny has gotten used to scrimping and saving as a way of life. But when it comes to business, you need to spend money to make money—like buying dozens of motels instead of just two. Mr. Rose would tell you that only by having faith in your own success can you achieve it.

Continental Cinnamon Buns

There's nothing like the smell of gooey, icing-topped cinnamon buns wafting through the air to entice customers to leave a nice five-star review. Of course, that scenario depends entirely on your family not pilfering the buns at every turn.

❯❯ MAKES 10 TO 12 BUNS

FOR THE ROLLS

2¾ cups all-purpose flour

¼ cup granulated sugar

½ teaspoon salt

1 (¼-ounce) packet instant yeast

½ cup whole milk

¼ cup water

3 tablespoons unsalted butter

1 large egg

FOR THE FILLING

3 tablespoons unsalted butter, softened

1 tablespoon ground cinnamon

¼ cup packed light or dark brown sugar

FOR THE ICING

1 cup confectioners' sugar

½ teaspoon pure vanilla extract

2 to 3 tablespoons whole milk

1. Lightly grease a 9-inch round cake pan. To make the rolls, in a large bowl, whisk together the flour, granulated sugar, salt, and yeast.

2. In another, heatproof bowl, combine the milk, water, and butter. Microwave in 30-second increments until the mixture is just warm. Then pour it into the bowl with the dry ingredients. Add the egg and stir until a soft dough forms.

3. Knead the dough on a lightly floured surface for 3 minutes, then transfer it to a lightly greased bowl, cover it loosely with plastic wrap, and let it rest for 10 minutes.

4. With a rolling pin, roll out the rested dough to a 14 x 8-inch rectangle. To make the filling, spread the softened butter over the dough. Combine the cinnamon and brown sugar in a small bowl and sprinkle it over the butter.

5. Roll the dough along the long edge to create a log, then slice the log into 10 to 12 even rolls. Place the rolls in the prepared pan. Cover the pan tightly with plastic wrap and allow the rolls to rise in a warm place for 1 to 1½ hours, or until doubled in size.

6. Preheat the oven to 375°F. Bake the rolls until lightly browned, 25 to 28 minutes. To make the icing, in a medium bowl, whisk together the confectioners' sugar, vanilla, and milk to achieve a pourable consistency. Spoon the icing over the warm rolls, and serve.

chapter

22

Grand OPENINGS

A grand opening can feel like the culmination of all your dreams and effort, but it's really just the beginning of a long (and hopefully wildly successful) journey. It's your chance to set a tone for your business that will carry it through years to come (and help you weed out the kind of off-brand customers who might be enticed by the heavy discounts of a soft launch). Knowing that this very personal project will be on full display for the judgment of others would give anyone crippling anxiety. But look how far you've come! Now is not the time to lose faith, because you've got a lot of shit to do to get this launch party off the ground. Now is the time to call the electrician, buy the cupcakes, and stock up on "loose-leaf tea."

DECIDING HOW TO LAUNCH

You've done the tireless work of bringing your business to fruition, from coming up with the concept and filing the first papers to putting up your shingle and wiring the lights. All that's left is to open the doors. It's your decision whether you want to shout your launch from the rooftops or whisper it in the ears of only the worthiest customers. But that decision should be based on your faith in the success of your business, not your fear of it. You've worked hard for this. You deserve to celebrate it.

The Firm Launch

Gwyneth may have gone with the soft launch, but that doesn't mean you have to follow her lead. As Johnny put it, "People love pizzazz." In a town starved for excitement, you probably won't need fireworks to pull off a truly grand opening. But putting a full-page ad in the paper might not be such a bad idea. You want to get people talking about the launch and ready to make a day of it, which means letting them know when it's happening and what fun things await them. Like wine. And suspiciously familiar-smelling loose-leaf tea.

The Soft Launch

When it comes to some events, the smaller, the better. A soft, invite-only launch makes your grand opening feel exclusive, which can generate even more interest than a firm launch. Create a select list of preapproved VIP guests and stick to that list when offering invitations. If you live in a small town, word will get out in no time and you'll arrive on opening day to find a line around the block. Except hopefully you won't be verbally assaulted by anyone like David is. You may have to put up with a few off-brand customers on Day 1, but they'll self-select out soon enough.

PREPARING FOR THE DAY

Once you've decided how you're going to launch, you need to start working toward it. You still have a ton of things to do before you can welcome your first customers, like stocking the shelves, ordering the wine, defending your decisions, installing the lights, and extending the invitations. Yes, you might need to watch a few YouTube tutorials and risk electrocution to get everything done. But it *will* get done.

Get Clear on Your Vision

During the lead up to the launch, you'll need to bring yourself back to your original concept over and over again. And not just when you need to shut up your newly minted businesswoman of a sister who won't stop quoting high school textbooks at you. Having a clear idea of the experience you hope to create will help you make purchases, create displays, *and* convince customers to fall in love with your business. It'll also help you maintain your composure when your parents offer unsolicited advice about your launch.

Plan for Success

You may be counting on sticking to your select guest list, but you need to plan like each VIP will be bringing their family of seventy-five. Because what if they do? The good news is, you can never have too much wine or too many cupcakes. If your business is a hit, your customers will go through the refreshments quickly. If it's a miss, *you* will go through the refreshments quickly. (It's an emotional day. David alone could probably clear a dozen cupcakes.)

To Discount or Not to Discount

A discount may feel meek for a grand opening, but it's a way to get people in the door who might be wary of a business that differs from their usual fare. Plus, there's no quicker way to start a queue than to make that discount "exclusive" in a town full of cheap locals with FOMO.

Don't Forget the Details

Equally as important as the food are those little details that customers count on, like working lights. Make sure that your business is physically ready for customers, from the sign above the door to the insurance that will save your ass if someone like Roland gets high on the loose-leaf tea and trips over a plunger. You can only do so much in a day, though, so ask your business partner for help when you need it.

❯❯ HAVE FAITH IN YOUR BUSINESS

Opening your own business can be as nerve-racking as it is exhilarating, and it's completely normal to have moments of doubt. But you have lived, eaten, and breathed this concept for months, and you know it will work. Now is the time to have faith. Whether that means putting on fireworks and throwing open the doors or inviting friends and family over for a first look is entirely up to you. But there's absolutely no need to be defeatist before you've even welcomed your first on-brand customer. Walk in with your head held high and get to fucking work.

❯❯ ENJOY THE MOMENT

After all the blood, sweat, and tears (so many tears) you've put into starting your own business, it can be all too easy to stay in go mode straight through the opening—especially if you're successful from the start. But you need to savor this accomplishment. If you don't have time during the day, take a moment after you put up the "Closed" sign for the first time. Look around at your business, breathe in the triumph of the day, give your business partner a long hug, and just imagine the success to come.

Customer Favorite Mini Cupcakes

What do you serve at a grand opening? Wine, obviously. But these bite-size vanilla cupcakes are the perfect treat to bring out the sweetness in the wine and keep customers from getting crumbs all over your products.

≫ MAKES 36 MINI CUPCAKES

FOR THE CUPCAKES

1¼ cups all-purpose flour

1¼ teaspoons baking powder

¼ teaspoon salt

4 tablespoons unsalted butter,
   at room temperature

¾ cup granulated sugar

2 large eggs

2 teaspoons pure vanilla extract

½ cup heavy cream

FOR THE BUTTERCREAM FROSTING

4 cups confectioners' sugar

½ cup unsalted butter, at room temperature

2 tablespoons heavy cream

2 teaspoons pure vanilla extract

1. Preheat the oven to 350°F and line a mini cupcake pan with mini cupcake liners. Depending on how many cupcakes your pan makes, you may need to bake in batches.

2. To make the cupcakes, in a small bowl, combine the flour, baking powder, and salt. Set aside.

3. In a stand mixer, or in a large bowl using a hand mixer, cream together the butter and granulated sugar. Beat in the eggs, one at a time, until combined, then mix in the vanilla. Gradually mix in a third of the dry ingredients followed by half of the heavy cream. Repeat with another third of the dry ingredients followed by the remaining heavy cream, then end with the remaining dry ingredients.

4. Spoon the batter into the prepared pan until each liner is half to two-thirds full. Bake the cupcakes for 12 to 15 minutes, or until a toothpick inserted into the center of a cupcake comes out dry. Transfer the baked cupcakes to a wire rack to cool. Repeat the process with another batch if necessary.

5. To make the frosting, in a stand mixer fitted with a whisk attachment, or in a large bowl using a hand mixer, combine the confectioners' sugar, butter, heavy cream, and vanilla until creamy. Add more heavy cream if the frosting is too thick.

6. Pipe or spread the frosting onto the cooled cupcakes and decorate them.

Disgruntled Pelican

Like David, the Disgruntled Pelican is a delightful mixture of sweet, tart, and spicy. Let this hypnotic cocktail soothe your nerves after an afternoon delight gone awry, or just sip it while enjoying all the charming awkwardness *Schitt's Creek* has to offer.

≫ SERVES 1

Ice cubes
1½ ounces smoky mezcal
2½ ounces grapefruit juice
¼ ounce lime juice
1 tablespoon grenadine
2–3 jalapeños

1. Fill a cocktail shaker with ice.

2. Add the mezcal, grapefruit juice, lime juice, and grenadine to the shaker, shake, and strain the mixture into a coupe glass.

3. Garnish with the jalapeños and enjoy.